Algeria

Algeria

BY MARTIN HINTZ

Enchantment of the World™
Second Series

CHILDREN'S PRESS®

An Imprint of Scholastic Inc.

Frontispiece: **Algiers**

Consultant: Frieda Ekotto, PhD, Chair, Department of Afroamerican and African Studies, University of Michigan, Ann Arbor, Michigan
Please note: All statistics are as up-to-date as possible at the time of publication.

Book production by The Design Lab

Library of Congress Cataloging-in-Publication Data
Names: Hintz, Martin, author.
Title: Algeria / by Martin Hintz.
Description: New York : Children's Press, [2017] | Series: Enchantment of the world
   | Includes bibliographical references and index.
Identifiers: LCCN 2016025107 | ISBN 9780531220818 (library binding)
Subjects: LCSH: Algeria—Juvenile literature.
Classification: LCC DT276 .H55 2017 | DDC 965—dc23
LC record available at https://lccn.loc.gov/2016025107

1 2 3 4 5 6 7 8 9 10 R 26 25 24 23 22 21 20 19 18 17

3 1907 00372 7822

Hands of a Tuareg woman

Contents

Left to right: **Coast, Guelma springs, flamingos, Tuareg, M'zab Valley**

CHAPTER 1

Welcome to Algeria

WOULD YOU LIKE TO TAKE A JOURNEY ACROSS Algeria? It is the largest country in Africa, so trekking across the country means a lot of walking. Perhaps a bus trip makes more sense, or even a drive along one of the newly opened freeways linking Algeria's main cities. Start off on the coast where the warm waters of the Mediterranean Sea lap sandy beaches. For a change to the old ways, switch to a slow camel ride to venture far to the south across the vast Sahara Desert. Or take a train from Algiers to Oran. Travel is even easier with the national airline Air Algérie, which flies passengers in comfort to many destinations.

Opposite: **Camels are well adapted to desert travel. The broad pads of their feet keep them from sinking into the sand, and they can go months without drinking water.**

ALGERIA

- ● Cities of more than 330,000 people
- ○ Other cities
- ✪ National capital

0   300 miles

0   300 kilometers

SPAIN

Mediterranean   Tizi   *S e a*

Gouraya N.P.

Taza   Skikda   Annaba   ITALY

N.P.

El Kala Nat'l. Park

Iles Habibas Marine Nature Reserve

Algiers   Ouzou

Mostaganem   Blida   Bejaïa

Kléber   Chlef   Djurdjura   Guelma

Chréa   Sétif   Constantine   Souk Ahras

Chélif   *Djurdjura N.P.*   M'Sila   *Belezma N.P.*   Oum el Bouaghi

Sidi Bel Abbès   Oran   Tiaret   *Theniet El Had N.P.*   Batna   Tébessa

Tlemcen   Saïda   Djelfa   Tolga   M'Chouneche

Messaad   Biskra

Mecheria   El Bayadh   Laghouat   El M'Ghair

TUNISIA

Aïn Sefra   El Oued

Ghardaïa   Touggourt

Beni Ounif   Kef el Guerrara

Béchar   Ouargla

Abadla   Hassi Messaoud

MOROCCO

Beni Abbès

Tabelbala   El Golea

Timimoun

Tindouf   LIBYA

W. Sahara   Adrar   I-n-Amenas

(MOROCCO)

Aoulef   I-n-Salah   Illizi

Chenachane   Reggane   *Tassili n'Ajjer National Park*

Arak

MAURITANIA   Djanet

I-n-Amguel

Ahaggar National Park

Tamanrasset

Algeria

Bordj Badji Mokhtar

MALI   Tin Zaouatine   NIGER

I-n-Guezzâm

N   W   E   S

Many journeys start in the colorful capital of Algiers. The city of more than two million has one of the best vistas in North Africa. Its tumble of houses and apartments blanket a rocky hillside overlooking the deep blue waters of the Mediterranean

People gather at a market in Ghardaïa, a town in the Sahara.

Sea. Not only is Algiers the center of Algerian politics, it is also the country's cultural hub, with many theaters, art galleries, and movie houses. The city offers an exciting mix of architecture, including French colonial neighborhoods from the 1800s and shiny, sun-catching domes on ancient mosques, Muslim houses of worship. People sometimes have to squeeze tightly through narrow alleys in the old district, the Kasbah, but they can stroll leisurely in the city's beautiful palm-fringed parks. The glittering Bay of Algiers provides a harbor for luxury yachts and sturdy freighters. Outdoor cafés are packed with businesspeople discussing their latest plans over tea. Kids run around everywhere, dashing out on errands or heading to school. The honks of car horns mingle with calls to prayer from mosque towers. The bustle of daily life is constant in Algiers.

**A man works in his
garden in Djanet, an
oasis in southeastern
Algeria. Most Algerians
who live in the Sahara
live in oases.**

It is quieter in the farm country outside the capital. Some
squat villages stand next to vineyards and vegetable gardens on
the flatlands along the seacoast. Others sit on the high plateaus
where sheep and goats bound over the rough terrain. Going
higher into the Atlas Mountains, the wind sings a cold, hard
song. On the far side of the peaks is the desert, with mile after
mile of barren rock and shifting dunes. The journey south from
Algiers takes travelers past ruins of ancient marble temples and
once-gilded palaces all the way to remote oases, where water
is more valuable than gold. In the desert, three-axle low-bed

Ruins still stand from the ancient city of Djemila, which the Romans founded about two thousand years ago. It is one of dozens of settlements the ancient Romans founded in what is now Algeria.

trailer trucks roar past lumbering camels. Freight is hauled along the long Trans-Sahara Highway all the way to the Niger border at I-n-Guezzâm.

Algeria has long been a crossroads of ideas, philosophies, dreams, and desires perfumed by the sweet scent of flowering jasmine and iris. Dirt-smudged oil field workers from dozens of countries mingle with nomadic herders. On city sidewalks, women in traditional clothing pass others wearing the latest European styles. Arabic, French, Tamazight, Chaouïa, and Tamahaq swirl in a heady mix of languages.

The lively beat of the city, the vibrant combination of cultures, and a fascinatingly varied landscape make Algerians proud of all their country has to offer.

CHAPTER 2

Land of Sun and Sand

ALGERIA BOASTS MANY DRAMATIC AND BEAUTIFUL landscapes, from the lovely Mediterranean coast to the steep Atlas Mountains to the immense Sahara Desert, with its shifting sand and searing sun.

Seven countries border Algeria. It shares its longest border—1,180 miles (1,900 kilometers)—with Morocco to the west. Western Sahara and Mauritania are also to the west; Mali and Niger lie to the south; and Libya and Tunisia to the east. The blue waters of the Mediterranean Sea lie to the north.

Algeria is the largest nation in Africa and the tenth-largest country in the world by area, covering 919,595 square miles (2,381,740 square kilometers). It is roughly 3.5 times the size of Texas.

Opposite: **Some parts of the Sahara are sandy, while other parts are covered in rock or gravel.**

Algeria's Geographic Features

Area: 919,595 square miles (2,381,740 sq km)

Lowest Elevation: Chott Melrhir, 131 feet (40 m) below sea level

Highest Elevation: Mount Tahat, 9,850 feet (3,002 m)

Greatest Distance East to West: 1,500 miles (2,400 km)

Greatest Distance North to South: 1,300 miles (2,100 km)

Length of Coastline: About 620 miles (1,000 km)

Longest River: Chelif, 450 miles (725 km)

Average Daily High Temperature: In Algiers, 62°F (17°C) in January, 90°F (32°C) in July; in Reggane, 73°F (23°C) in January, 116°F (47°C) in July

Average Daily Low Temperature: In Algiers, 42°F (6°C) in January, 67°F (19°C) in July; in Reggane, 49°F (9°C) in January, 91°F (33°C) in July

Average Annual Precipitation: 8 to 16 inches (20 to 40 cm); less than 5 inches (13 cm) in the Sahara

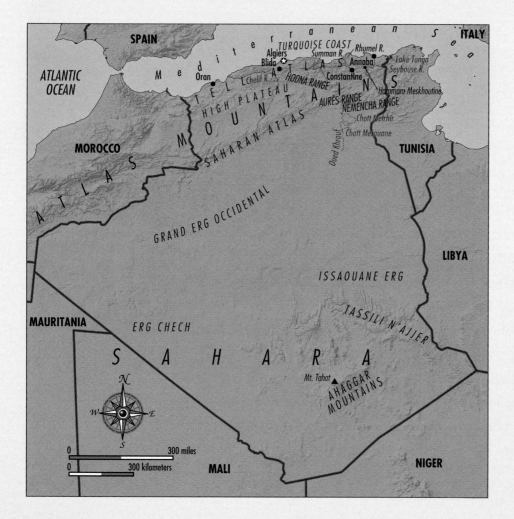

Lay of the Land

Two adjectives describe much of Algeria's landscape: dry and windswept. Barely 3 percent of the land is arable, or good for agriculture. This farmland is found along the coastline. Another 13 percent is suitable for grazing animals, and some 2 percent of the countryside is thickly forested. Then there is the sand—lots of it.

Algeria can be divided into two large areas. The mountains, plains, and plateaus of the north are called the Tell. To the south lies the great Sahara Desert.

North-central Algeria stretches along the Mediterranean coast and includes crowded, lively Algiers. The country has about 620 miles (1,000 km) of coastline. Many of the best

Buildings line the hills overlooking the turquoise waters of the Mediterranean Sea.

swimming beaches are near Algiers and to the east along the Turquoise Coast. The coast sometimes experiences fierce winter storms with high seas and raging winds.

Northeastern Algeria features towering mountains, including the Aurès, the Hodna, and the Nemencha Ranges. Inland from the mountains are flat plains where fields of grain grow. The Tell Atlas rises in northwestern Algeria. South of this range is the High Plateau, which is marked by broad, dry, rolling plains. Farther south is the steep Saharan Atlas, a mountain range that runs all the way across Algeria from east to west.

The Atlas Mountains are dry and rugged, with few trees.

Sandy Land

Say the word *desert*, and people usually think of sand. Not all deserts have sand, but the Sahara has plenty of it.

An erg is a sea of moving sand with little or no vegetation. The Issaouane Erg in eastern Algeria is so vast it can be seen from the International Space Station. It covers more than 14,000 square miles (36,260 sq km).

Deserts can feature several types of sand dunes. A barchan is a crescent-shaped dune, that is formed when the wind blows consistently in one direction. This produces one steep side to the dune and a wide, sloping front. As sand falls down the front of the dune, the barchan continually moves forward. Where the wind changes direction, dunes form an extensive, curving pattern called a *seif* in Arabic. The word means "sword" because the dune looks like an ancient sword called a scimitar. A third pattern results when the wind blows

from all directions. While the sand does not move much, it forms a star-shaped pattern with arms extending for miles. Saharan winds can also scour an area clear of sand, leaving bare rock or gravel.

The Saharan Atlas marks the northern rim of the vast Sahara Desert. The Sahara covers about 80 percent of Algeria. Some parts of the Sahara consist of sand dunes. Other parts are rocky land. In Algeria's southern Sahara rise the Ahaggar Mountains. These jagged, rocky peaks include Algeria's highest point, Mount Tahat, which rises 9,850 feet (3,002 meters) above sea level.

River, Lake, and Spring

Algeria is an arid land. Most rivers are short, and many dry up for part of the year. The nation's longest river is the Chelif, which flows 450 miles (725 km) down from the rugged

The Rhumel River has cut deep into the land near Constantine, in northern Algiera.

Atlas Mountains to the sea. Other important rivers are the Seybouse, the Summan, and the Rhumel.

Welcome Water

Across Algeria's arid land are oases, places in the desert where water rises from deep underground. These palm-ringed oases are sometimes called the Soul of Algeria for their life-giving pools of fresh water. Among the best known is Touggourt in the northern Sahara. It has a population of 153,000, and its main industry is growing date palms. Farther south is Hassi Messaoud. Once a layover for camel caravans, it is now a bustling city of 60,000 with an international airport that serves workers in nearby oil and gas fields.

There are few freshwater lakes in Algeria, but there are salt lakes called *chotts*. Many chotts are located in the semidesert plateaus high in the Atlas Mountain range, while others are in the far south. The country's lowest point is Chott Melrhir in northeastern Algeria at 131 feet (40 m) below sea level. Its size varies from season to season depending on how much of its water has evaporated. At its peak size, it sprawls over about 2,600 square miles (6,700 sq km).

Algeria also has some 240 geothermal and mineral springs, mostly in the northeast. For centuries, Algerians have used these mineral waters to help treat skin diseases and disorders.

Hot and Dry

Algeria's climate varies from region to region depending on elevation and distance from the sea. The north has a pleasant Mediterranean climate. In Algiers, temperatures reach an average daily high of about 90 degrees Fahrenheit (32 degrees

Celsius) in July and 62°F (17°C) in January. Spring and summer are perfect for enjoying outdoor activities and relaxing in open-air cafés. In the Sahara, however, temperatures often top 115°F (46°C), with extreme highs reaching above 120°F (49°C). This is one of the earth's harshest environments.

Algeria receives relatively little precipitation. The average annual rainfall in Algiers is 27 inches (69 centimeters). The driest month is July, with only 0.1 inch (2.5 millimeters) of precipitation. The wettest month is December, when the region gets an average of 5 inches (13 cm) of rainfall. This

Sunbathers and their colorful umbrellas fill a beach in Algiers.

A Look at Algeria's Cities

The largest city in Algeria is its capital, Algiers, which is home to more than two million people. The second-largest is Oran (below), with a population that tops eight hundred thousand. In precolonial times, the city's name was Wahran, which means "lions." Legend says two of these big cats were killed near the city around 900 BCE. Their statues stand outside the city hall in Place du 1er Novembre. Oran is located on the coast west of Algiers. The city was founded around 937 CE by Spanish Muslims, called Moors. Oran is filled with French colonial buildings, and some Algerians call it the second Paris. The downtown is crowded with high-end retail stores, banks, apartments, and office buildings. An imposing structure from the 1700s is the Bey Othmane Mosque. A multitude of nightclubs and cabarets line the seafront strip called La Corniche. The upbeat city is noted for stylish high fashion and dancing to the beat of raï, Algeria's national music. Oran is a major commercial center in Algeria, and many oil companies have offices there. The city's location on the Mediterranean makes it an important transportation hub, with ferry service to France and Spain.

Constantine (above) is Algeria's third-largest city, with about 450,000 residents. Many people consider

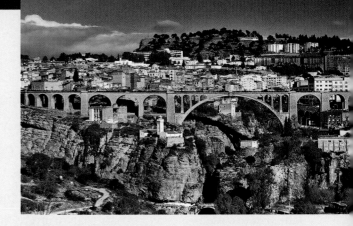

Constantine one of the most beautiful cities on the planet. Seven bridges cross a deep ravine where the Rhumel River flows. The crevasse is between 500 and 1,000 feet (150 and 300 m) deep, and at one time helped protect the city from invaders. Now the site is a hot spot for photographers. Sturdy homes cling to the sides of the cliffs. More than two thousand years ago, Constantine, then called Cirta, was the capital of a kingdom called Numidia. After it was taken over by the Romans, however, it was renamed for the Roman emperor Constantine. The city is the center of Algerian grain trade and has factories that produce textiles, leather goods, and tractors. Among Constantine's landmarks are the palace of Ahmed Bey and a Roman aqueduct that once carried water to the fortress.

Annaba, with more than three hundred thousand residents, is Algeria's fourth-largest city. It lies in the east, near the Tunisian border. It has some of the best swimming beaches on the Mediterranean and is a good harbor. Many different cultures have settled there. The Phoenicians arrived in the twelfth century BCE. Over the centuries, the city was passed to the Romans, the Vandals, the Arabs, the Turks, and the French. Today, Annaba is a center of the steel industry, home to the El Hadjar steel manufacturing complex, the largest in Africa.

Land of Sun and Sand **23**

helps fill the country's small streams, which usually dry up in the summer. Many parts of the Sahara receive less than 1 inch (2.5 cm) of rain per year.

A wind called the sirocco sometimes blows north from the heart of the Sahara. This humid wind blows choking reddish grit angrily across the Mediterranean to Europe. Mixed with moisture drawn from the sea, the resulting "red rain" can damage machinery, magnify health problems, and cause

Pedestrians need their umbrellas on a rainy March day in Algiers. Rain falls in the city an average of once every three days in the spring.

dangerous driving conditions. When the sirocco is blowing, sometimes it is difficult to see even 100 feet (30 m) in any direction.

Sandstorms can occur any time of year but are most common in the spring.

Shaking Land

Destructive earthquakes are a fact of Algerian life, particularly in the northern districts. They are caused when the giant tectonic plates that make up earth's outer layer begin to shift. A terrible quake rocked the Algiers region in May 1716, killing upward of twenty thousand people. More recently, a quake in 1980 left five thousand dead. Another in 2003 killed more than two thousand people and injured another ten thousand. Undersea quakes in the Mediterranean also occur. Some have caused large tsunami waves that have swept over beaches, damaging harbors and sinking boats.

Land of Sun and Sand **25**

CHAPTER 3

Natural Algeria

THE NATURAL WORLD IN ALGERIA IS A MIX OF PRIME agricultural land north of the Saharan Atlas Mountains and rugged plants and animals living in the harsher landscape south of the jagged peaks. Despite centuries of deforestation and overgrazing, there are least 3,100 types of plants in Algeria.

Plant Life

Northern Algeria's climate is much like that of southern Europe. As such, similar vegetation grows in both locales. Towering cork trees grow well in the dry soil. Their thick bark is used for making wine bottle corks and bulletin boards. Scattered patches of forests grow in the higher Tell Atlas and Saharan Atlas. Some common trees there are pine, ash, juniper, and pungent Atlas cedar. While much of the High Plateau is barren, tracts of esparto grass and brushwood survive there. More than 160 species of plants grow in the Sahara. Drought-resistant grasses and acacia and jujube trees are among the hardiest.

Date palms have been cultivated for more than five thousand years. Prized for their fruit, they are highly valued in Algeria, where about eighteen million of these trees grow.

Donkeys rest in the shade of an acacia tree.

Algeria's National Animal

The creamy-colored fennec fox is Algeria's national animal. It lives in the Sahara, digging dens in the sand for protection. The fennec has many adaptations that enable it to live in the desert. Its large ears help disperse heat. The soles of its paws are covered with thick fur, protecting its feet as it runs across the hot land. Fennecs are nocturnal, coming out only at night to hunt. Meals consist of birds, small mammals, eggs, and insects. The foxes are tiny, weighing 1 to 3 pounds (0.5 to 1.5 kilograms). They are playful, making purring sounds like a cat if they are happy and snarling if upset. *Les Fennecs* is the nickname of the Algerian national soccer team. Just like a good soccer player, the fennec can jump, twist around, and move quickly after its prey.

They tower about 75 feet (23 m) high and need full sun and sizzling heat to thrive. This makes them perfect for oases, where their roots descend deep into the sandy soil. Harvesters used to scamper up the trunks and pluck dates with forked sticks, then lower the fruit to the ground. Mechanical pickers now make the job easier.

Many Animals

Algeria is home to a wide range of animals, small and large. Among the small creatures are the spiny mouse, the Algerian gerbil, and Savigny's fringe-fingered lizard. Butterflies, ants, beetles, and mosquitoes are common. Locusts, a kind of grasshopper, can be a problem, swarming over fields and eating everything they can. Four species of scorpions live in Algeria, and they are

Scorpions sting thousands of people every year in the desert and mountains of Algeria. The stings are particularly dangerous to young children.

among the country's most dangerous creatures. They live underground, emerging at night to eat bugs, worms, rodents, and even snakes. Scorpions can be small, typically from 1 to 6 inches (2.5 to 15 cm) long, but the venom they carry in their tails can be deadly. People in the desert shake out their shoes before putting them on in the morning and never stick unprotected hands into any dark places where scorpions might lurk.

Larger animals found on Algeria's plains, mountains, and deserts include ibex, boars, jackals, hares, and antelope. One interesting species is the jerboa, a rodent that looks like a tiny kangaroo. When pursued by hungry predators, the jerboa can hop as fast as 15 miles per hour (25 kph). The reclusive Saharan cheetah was first photographed in the highlands

Ships of the Desert

The camel is a symbol of the desert. The lumbering beasts can travel 25 miles (40 km) a day. They can slurp 30 gallons (114 liters) of water in ten minutes and then go for days without another drink. The camel's flaring nostrils and long, thick eyelashes keep the blowing sand at bay. For hundreds of years, desert dwellers such as the Tuareg used camels as beasts of burden. But four-wheel-drive trucks are becoming more common as cargo carriers. Today, people riding camels are likely to be tourists.

of southern Algeria in the late 2000s. It is one of the most endangered animals in the world. Only about 250 survive anywhere in the world. Another rare animal is Cuvier's gazelle. Only about five hundred remain in Algeria. These gazelles scamper fearlessly around the boulders and brush of the Atlas Mountains. Well adapted to dry habitats, they get most of

Both male and female Cuvier's gazelles have horns, but the males' horns are longer and have more prominent ridges.

The Barb

A northern African breed of horse, the Barb (or Berber) is prized for being hardy and having great stamina. It is an excitable horse and, therefore, a challenge to tame. The Barb was bred for usefulness and endurance. It has a strong body and strong feet. It is noted for its ability to coil and wheel around, making it the perfect animal for use in mounted warfare.

their water from grazing on plants. Unfortunately, poachers (illegal hunters) often kill the gazelles for their hides and meat by firing at them with machine guns.

Other species are at even greater risk. Among the country's most endangered animal is the serval. This feline is larger than a housecat but smaller than a leopard. The serval has the longest legs in the cat family and sports a spotted pelt. However, only a few of these elegant creatures still exist.

Other creatures, such as the scimitar oryx and the dama gazelle, disappeared from Algeria entirely by the 1990s because of overhunting and the loss of grazing lands. The elegant, dark-maned Barbary lion has also disappeared.

Bird Life

About four hundred bird species live in Algeria at least part of the year. The rare Algerian nuthatch and Audouin's gull are among them. Waterbirds such as marbled teals and white-headed ducks can be found in the marshes around Lake Tonga. Flamingos love the shallow pools of the Chott Merouane and Oued Khrouf, south of Biskra. The gangly birds are also found in the eastern part of the High Plateau. Coots and geese can also be found scurrying around the wetlands. The northern bald ibis stands 2.5 feet (75 cm) tall, with a wingspan that can be 4 feet (1.2 m) wide. They have curved, narrow beaks that they use to grub for food in the marshes. But illegal hunting, climate change, and habitat destruction threaten these birds in their western Sahara home.

Flamingos wade along a beach in Algeria. Their diet consists of shrimp, algae, and other nutrients they find in the mud.

Birds that prefer dry land include the woodcock and Barbary partridge. The scarce houbara bustard lives in open dry areas where it can easily hunt, but where it can also be easily preyed upon. Houbara bustards need to look out for hungry raptors such as golden eagles, vultures, falcons, and hawks.

Monk seals live in the Mediterranean Sea and along part of the Atlantic coast of North Africa.

Life in the Water

The Mediterranean is rich in sea creatures. The reclusive Mediterranean monk seal lives in caves along the rocky coast-

line. Fishers sometimes kill the seals because they compete for fish. Some monk seals also become tangled in nets and drown. These circumstances and pollution have caused seals to be placed on the endangered species list.

Algeria boasts thirty-nine species of freshwater fish. Reservoirs and rivers are the natural habitat of the colorful barb fish. Carp, catfish, sturgeon, pike, and mullet often go into an Algerian stewpot. The tiny killifish lives in salt marshes and coastal lagoons. Fish can even be found in the Sahara. The waters of Ahaggar National Park are home to the desert barbel, a cousin of the carp. Aquaculture, or fish farming, is a growing business in Algeria. There are farms for shrimp, clams, carp, eels, mullet, and more.

Protecting Wildlife

In an effort to preserve nature, Algeria launched its first hunting and environmental protection laws in the early 1980s. Since then, the government has established lists of protected animals and plants. Algeria has also established preserves throughout the country.

Tassili n'Ajjer National Park is home to exquisite Saharan myrtle and Saharan cypress and numerous endangered animals. El Kala, Gouraya, and Taza National Parks on the coast focus on saving plants and wildlife native to that area. Theniet El Had and Djurdjura National Parks are two of Algeria's six mountainous reserves. The Îles Habibas Marine Nature Reserve (left) protects several small islands 14 miles (22 km) from the coast.

CHAPTER 4

Out of the Past

MILLIONS OF YEARS AGO, THE REGION THAT IS now Algeria looked extremely different than it does today. Creatures such as giant piglike moeritheriums roamed through what was then a fertile, lush landscape.

Much later, hundreds of thousands of years ago, early nomadic hunters were attracted to the rich wildlife in the region. Algeria abounds in cave art depicting these hunts. Boulders and rock walls in the Tassili n'Ajjer, a wide plateau in southeast Algeria, are covered with thousands of such paintings and engravings. Some of this art dates back ten thousand years. Like a book, they showcase changes in climate, animal migrations, and everyday human life.

Opposite: **Rock drawings found at Tassili n'Ajjer in the Sahara date from 5000 BCE.**

The Berber Numidian people built a huge royal tomb near the Mediterranean coast about two thousand years ago.

The Berbers

People called Berbers were the first to claim the region that is now Algeria as their permanent home. The climate changed around 2000 BCE. Drought savaged the land, and the large animals that had once lived in the region disappeared. But the Berbers remained in North Africa, living in scattered settlements. They dramatically changed their lifestyle in response to the drier climate. They either dug deeper wells or roamed the desolate landscape looking for oases with water. They used camels as transportation, moving slowly across the desert land.

Traders and Invaders

Over the centuries, explorers from other lands arrived. Among them were the Phoenicians, who were based in the eastern Mediterranean. They established coastal outposts in what is now Algeria by 1100 BCE. Trade goods flowed out from Africa's interior to Mediterranean harbor cities, making them wealthy. In the 800s BCE, Carthage, a city founded by the Phoenicians in what is now Tunisia, sent commercial vessels to far-flung lands. In Algeria, the Carthaginians established settlements at sites such as Tipasa and Hippo Regius, today's Annaba.

Carthage was in competition with the Roman Republic. The two powers faced off in three conflicts called the Punic Wars. From 264 to 146 BCE, North Africa and southern Europe were ravaged by marching armies. In the second century BCE, Masinissa, the leader of a Berber kingdom called Numidia, joined forces with the Romans. Carthage was eventually defeated, giving Rome undisputed power in North Africa. Roman fields and vineyards flourished, and slaves, grain, marble, and gold were sent back to Italy.

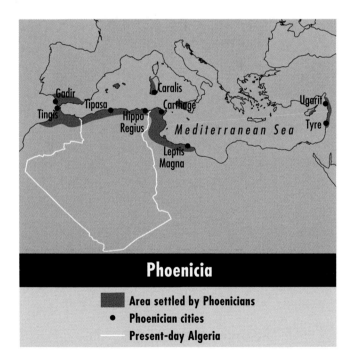

Rome's control of North Africa did not last. Over the centuries, it became more difficult for the Romans to maintain power over their vast empire. Among the groups attacking a weakened Rome were the Vandals.

The Roman fleet sinks Carthaginian ships during a battle in the Mediterranean during the First Punic War in 256 BCE.

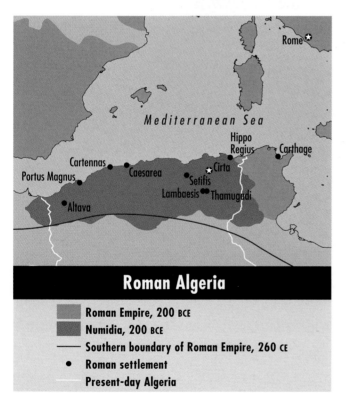

Rome ⭐

Mediterranean Sea

Hippo Regius • Carthage

Cartennas
Portus Magnus • Caesarea • ⭐Cirta
• Setifis
Lambaesis •• Thamugadi

• Altava

Roman Algeria

Roman Empire, 200 BCE
Numidia, 200 BCE
— Southern boundary of Roman Empire, 260 CE
• Roman settlement
— Present-day Algeria

They stormed out of eastern Europe, fighting their way south and eventually making their way across the Mediterranean into Africa around 429 CE. Their burning and raiding led to the word *vandalize*, meaning to deliberately destroy something. The Vandals soon gained control of coastal Numidia.

Because of its location, Algeria was in the center of all this turmoil. The next invaders were the Byzantines, from what is now Turkey and Greece. They thrashed the Vandals in 533 and drove them out of the region by the following year.

Arabs Arrive

The Byzantine reign came to a halt in the 600s when Arabs stormed across the landscape from strongholds in the Arabian Peninsula. They brought with them a new religion—Islam. The people they conquered were encouraged to become Muslims, followers of Islam. By the eighth century, most Berbers had converted from their traditional beliefs.

The Rustamid dynasty founded the first Muslim state in Algeria in 777. Other Arab dynasties, including the Fatimids, the Almoravids, and the Almohads, followed.

At its height, the Roman city of Timgad was home to fifteen thousand people. The city was attacked by Vandals in the 400s and later by other groups before finally being abandoned in the 700s.

Khayr al-Din helped the Ottoman Turks gain control over the Mediterranean.

Pirates on the Seas

By the fifteenth and sixteenth centuries, the Spanish from the west and the Ottoman Turks from the east eagerly expanded into the territory of northern Africa. The two groups vied for possession of the area, and the Turks were the ultimate winners. They were led by the skilled fighter Khayr al-Din (ca. 1466–1546), a noted admiral. His nickname was Barbarossa, meaning "red beard" in Italian. Barbarossa allowed pirates, called corsairs, to hole up along the North African coast. They became known as the Barbary pirates because Europeans called the North African coast the Barbary Coast. The Barbary pirates raided ships far out into the Mediterranean for the next three hundred years.

Turkish Government

The Turks were skilled rulers, establishing an intricate system for effective government. At the height of power was the sultan, who used governors called pashas to keep watch over the local people. The Turkish administration was propped up by the ojaq, an elite military unit known for its ruthlessness. The ojaqs became unhappy with how they were treated so they revolted in 1671. They murdered their officers and appointed their own ruler, called a dey. This coveted position was dangerous to hold. Over the next century, fourteen deys were assassinated as they fought over the region's wealth.

Slaves were a major commodity among the corsairs in Algeria at this time. Captured sailors were sold into captivity, as were residents of raided seaside villages. Slaves without special skills worked in quarries, labored on farms, or rowed pirate ships. Many were worked to death. As a result, a fresh supply of victims was always needed. Enslaved carpenters, blacksmiths, and other skilled tradespeople were often spared this fate. Many were treated well and some were freed. Some people paid ransom to the corsairs to release captives. In Europe, priests raised money and traveled to Algeria to purchase as many Christians as possible to set them free. This was so lucrative for the pirates that they left the priests alone. The corsairs sat back and counted their reward money.

It is estimated that around a million Protestants, Catholics, Jews, and Muslims were bought and sold in Algiers's slave markets from the 1500s to the 1700s. At the same time, Europeans regularly enslaved captured Muslims.

Many nations paid the corsairs tribute, or bribes, so their ships would not be attacked. Even the young United States paid bribes. Eventually, enough was enough. The United States fought the Barbary states of North Africa in two wars

American soldiers board a Barbary gunboat during the war between the United States and the Barbary states in the early 1800s.

between 1801 and 1815. By the time the second war ended, the United States was no longer paying tribute to the corsairs, and piracy soon faded in the region.

The French Arrive

In the 1820s, the unpopular French king Charles X needed to divert his citizens' attention from economic problems. Piracy in the Mediterranean provided the opportunity. In 1827, a dey and a French consul in Algiers got into an argument over paying tribute. The dey swatted the French official with a fly whisk, a grievous insult. This gave the French an excuse to invade Algeria. Although the French gained control of the region, the Algerians continued to fight. In the 1840s, the Arab leader Abd al-Qadir led an uprising against the French, making him a hero in Algerian history. But Abd al-Qadir was forced to surrender in 1847, and the following year Algeria became a province of France.

Thousands of French settlers, called *colons* or *pieds-noirs*, settled in Algeria. Many of the newcomers became farmers and

A French family stands outside their house in Miliana, southwest of Algiers. By the early twentieth century, more than half a million French people lived in Algeria.

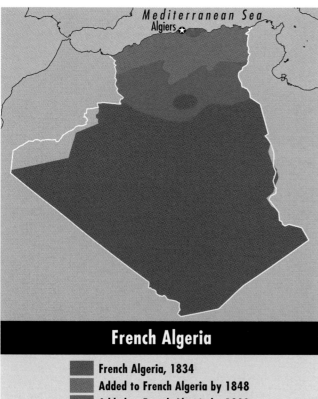

French Algeria

- French Algeria, 1834
- Added to French Algeria by 1848
- Added to French Algeria by 1900
- Added to French Algeria by 1934
- Present-day Algeria

business owners, but the Algerians themselves had little control over their own government and economy.

Time of War

From 1914 to 1918, World War I raged. Many Algerian soldiers fought on the side of France during the war. After the war, a strong Algerian resistance movement to French colonial authority began.

Nazi Germany invaded and occupied France during World War II, which began in 1939. French officials working for the Germans set up a puppet French government in the city of Vichy, France. During the war, Algerian nationalism gained strength, but the Vichy government

ignored Algerian demands for more freedom. Thousands of Algerians fought on the side of the Free French, who were French soldiers fighting to defeat Germany.

During the war, Algeria became a central location for various military groups. In 1942, British, American, and Free French armies invaded Algeria. They soon took control of the region. The Allies—the countries fighting Nazi Germany—moved their North African headquarters to Algiers. Beginning in May 1943, the Free French government was also based in Algiers. The head of the Allied army, U.S. general Dwight D. Eisenhower, lived in Algiers for several months before the Allied invasion of Europe in 1944. His busy office was in the city's historic St. George Hotel.

Two Algerian soldiers stand with a French soldier (right) during World War I. About 170,000 Algerians served in the French army during the war.

In 1960, Algerians fill the streets of Algiers at a demonstration demanding independence.

Fighting for Independence

The Allies defeated the Nazis in 1945. The victory encouraged Algerians to press for their own independence. The French colonists were frightened that they might lose control of their adopted country. Political reforms meant to give more power to native Algerians were rejected, causing increased tensions. A revolution led by the Algerian National Liberation Front (FLN) began in 1954 and wore on for seven years. Hundreds of thousands of Algerians were killed in bombings, assassinations, and street fights. French forces fought fiercely and often tortured captured revolutionaries. The French public was horrified at the army's rough actions, and support for the colonists waned. However, France's military commanders in Algeria wanted to keep the region French, and in 1961 they revolted against French moves toward Algerian independence.

But the French government finally had enough of the bloodshed, and after intense negotiations it was agreed that Algerians would vote on their future. On July 1, 1962, six million Algerians cast ballots in favor of independence. Four days later, Algeria became an independent nation. In the aftermath of these changes, about eight hundred thousand Algerians of European descent left the new country. They feared they would be blamed for the French military's mistreatment of Algerians.

The Young Country

Ahmed Ben Bella, who had fought with the Free French in World War II, became Algeria's first president after independence. He favored state control of industry and business and encouraged poor Algerians to confiscate land owned by the colonists. Army commander Houari Boumedienne overthrew Ben Bella in 1965 and led the country until his death in 1978. Under his rule, Algeria took over French oil fields in the Sahara and increased state control over the economy. Boumedienne was succeeded by Chadli Bendjedid who reversed course and allowed private business to flourish in Algeria.

By the mid-1980s, Algeria's economy was in dire trouble. Many Algerians thought the nation's politicians were corrupt. Deadly riots erupted around the country, with people demanding a cleansing of the government. They succeeded in changing the constitution to allow other political parties to organize. Until that time, the FLN was the only political party allowed.

A member of the Islamic Salvation Front holds up a Qur'an during a demonstration in 1991.

Elections were held in December 1991, and the Islamic Salvation Front (FIS) won 47 percent of the vote. Another round of elections was scheduled for January 1992, and the FIS was expected to do well. Fearing that Algeria would become an Islamic state, the army forced Bendjedid out of office, and the election was canceled. The FIS was outlawed, and many of its supporters were jailed. Violence ripped through Algeria, resulting in more than 150,000 deaths by the end of the 1990s. Many Algerians fled to France, where they hoped to escape the strife and find a better economic future.

Troubled Times

General Liamine Zeroual was appointed president in 1994. He tried to broker a peace agreement between the army and the FIS, but his efforts collapsed. Abdelaziz Bouteflika was elected president in 1999. Bouteflika was the army's favorite politician, and many ordinary Algerians thought his election was a sham. As a result, Islamic rebels launched a war against the government, and there were many deaths on both sides. The civil war eventually wound down. In 2005, brave Algerians

Abdelaziz Bouteflika served in the National Liberation Army during the fight for Algerian independence. After independence, he joined the government, eventually serving nearly twenty years as foreign minister.

agreed to pardon both the military and the rebels for many of the crimes committed during the uprising. Most members of the FIS accepted the pardons and blended back into Algerian society.

Revolutionary leader Ben Bella died at age ninety-five in 2012, the year marking the fiftieth anniversary of Algeria's independence from France. That same year, national elections took place with forty-four parties and 186 independent candidates. It was the first election since the Arab Spring, a wave of protests in support of democracy that had swept the Muslim

In 1998, many Algerian villagers felt threatened by the Islamic Salvation Front, so they armed themselves to fight.

world, deposing several dictators. But many Algerians chose not to vote in the election. They were disgusted with the country's legislature, which they felt was just for show. They believed the real power resided with the military. Bouteflika was elected to his fourth term of office in 2014, despite not campaigning and rarely appearing in public since suffering a stroke in 2013. Many Algerians believe that Bouteflika's younger brother Saïd is actually in charge.

In 2011, Algerians took to the streets, demanding greater freedom and democracy. Although the demonstrations were banned, young people continued to protest.

CHAPTER 5

Government Today

ALGERIA IS A PRESIDENTIAL REPUBLIC, A FORM of government in which the leader is a president rather than a king, and citizens express their will through elected representatives. The country's current constitution was adopted in 1976 and has been updated regularly since then. In 1996, the document was changed to allow the formation of political parties not founded on "religious, linguistic, racial, sex, corporatist or regional basis." The Ministry of the Interior, however, must approve all political parties.

In response to the Arab Spring uprisings in the Middle East and North Africa in 2011, President Abdelaziz Bouteflika promised to alter the constitution in response to some of the

Opposite: **An Algerian woman casts a ballot during an election.**

people's concerns. After much discussion, changes were made in 2016. These changes include limiting the president to two five-year terms, blocking Algerians with dual nationality from running for high government positions, and ensuring a free press and freedom of assembly. Tamazight, a language spoken by Algeria's Berber population, was also recognized as an official language, along with Arabic.

Algeria's National Government

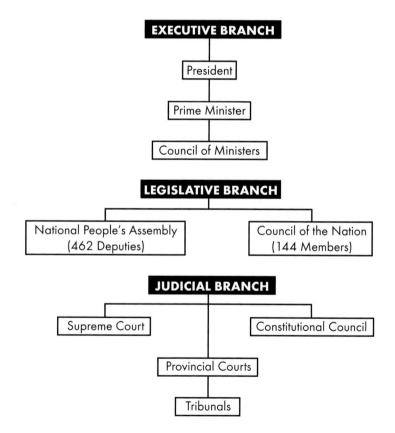

EXECUTIVE BRANCH

President

Prime Minister

Council of Ministers

LEGISLATIVE BRANCH

National People's Assembly (462 Deputies)

Council of the Nation (144 Members)

JUDICIAL BRANCH

Supreme Court

Constitutional Council

Provincial Courts

Tribunals

Abdelmalek Sellal, a member of the National Liberation Front, became prime minister in 2014.

Running the Government

Algeria has three branches of government: executive, legislative, and judicial. The president is the head of the executive branch. The president must be a Muslim, a native Algerian, and at least forty years old. The president's spouse must also be Algerian. The president leads the High Security Council, making him or her responsible for the country's defense. Other duties of the president include appointing important officials, including judges and the chair of the Bank of Algeria.

Another important presidential responsibility is naming the prime minister, who serves a five-year term as the head of the cabinet, called the Council of Ministers. The prime minister directs government operations. However, if Algeria's legislature does not support the prime minister, he or she has to resign and the president must name another person as prime minister.

Members of the National Assembly raise their hands to vote. About 30 percent of the members of the National Assembly are women.

The Council of Ministers is the country's chief executive body, managing government's day-to-day operations. Among the departments are the Ministry for Youth and Sports, the Ministry for Finance, the Ministry for Energy and Mines, and the Ministry for Foreign Affairs. The prime minister appoints members of the council.

Algeria's parliament has two branches. The National People's Assembly has 462 members. Each representative is elected by popular vote for a five-year term and can be reelected. The other branch is the senate, called the Council of the Nation, which has 144 members who serve six-year terms. One-third are appointed by the president. The remaining two-thirds are elected by regional and municipal authorities.

In recent years, many different political parties have arisen in Algeria. Twenty-eight of them are represented in

National Flag

The Algerian national flag features two equal vertical bands of green and white. A red, five-pointed star within a red crescent is centered over the boundary of the vertical bands. The colors are symbolic: Green represents Islam, white denotes purity, and red indicates peace and liberty. The white portion also calls to mind the banner carried by revolutionary leader Abd al-Qadir in battles against the French in the 1800s. The crescent and star are Islamic symbols. The flag was flown by the National Liberation Front in 1954 and was officially adopted as the national flag when independence was declared in 1962.

the National People's Assembly. Among these are the president's National Liberation Front (FLN), the Algerian Popular Movement, the National Republican Alliance, New Dawn, the Socialist Forces Front, the Movement of Society for Peace, and the Rally for Culture and Democracy.

The Judicial System

The highest court in Algeria is the Supreme Court. Its members hear appeals of cases tried in lower courts. Supreme Court judges are appointed by the High Council of Magistracy, an administrative body presided over by the president. Beneath the Supreme Court are lower courts. Provincial courts hear criminal cases and appeals, while tribunals focus on civil and commercial cases. Algeria also has a nine-member Constitutional Council that rules on the constitutionality of treaties and other international matters.

President Abdelaziz Bouteflika greets judges at the beginning of the judicial year. The number of female lawyers in Algeria has risen steadily and women now account for about two-thirds of all judges in the country.

Defendants in civilian courts are allowed a public trial, the right to a lawyer, the right to confront witnesses, and the right of appeal.

Military

Algeria has the largest defense budget of any nation in Africa. Its military consists of the People's National Army, the Algerian National Navy, the Algerian Air Force, and the Territorial Air Defense Forces. All men over age nineteen must serve in the military for at least eighteen months.

The military plays a large role in Algerian politics. Its elite officers have frequently spoken out on political and social issues. This boldness has often caused challenges for the civilian government. In 2015, President Bouteflika removed

National Anthem

Algeria's national anthem is "Kassaman," or "Quassaman" ("We Pledge"). Mufdi Zakariah wrote the lyrics in 1956 while he was imprisoned by French colonial forces. The music is by Egyptian composer Mohamed Fawzi. Algeria adopted the song as its national anthem in 1962.

English translation

We swear by the lightning that destroys,
By the streams of generous blood being shed,
By the bright flags that wave,
Flying proudly on the high mountains,
That we are in revolt, whether to live or to die,

We are determined that Algeria should live,
So be our witness—be our witness—be our witness!

We are soldiers in revolt for truth
And we have fought for our independence.
When we spoke, nobody listened to us,
So we have taken the noise of gunpowder as our rhythm
And the sound of machine guns as our melody,

We are determined that Algeria should live,
So be our witness—be our witness—be our witness!

O France!
Past is the time of palavers
We closed it as we close a book
O France!
The day to settle the accounts has come!
Prepare yourself! Here is our answer!
The verdict, our Revolution will return it
We are determined that Algeria should live,
So be our witness—be our witness—be our witness!

From our heroes we shall make an army come to being,
From our dead we shall build up a glory,
Our spirits shall ascend to immortality
And on our shoulders we shall raise the Standard.
To the nation's Liberation Front we have sworn an oath,

We are determined that Algeria should live,
So be our witness—be our witness—be our witness!

The cry of the Fatherland sounds from the battlefields.
Listen to it and answer the call!
Let it be written with the blood of martyrs
And be read to future generations.
Oh, Glory, we have held out our hand to you,

We are determined that Algeria should live,
So be our witness—be our witness—be our witness!

Algerian soldiers guard natural gas facilities in the desert. About half a million people serve in the Algerian military.

several generals he thought might become a threat to his power. Early in 2016, he also dissolved the Department of Intelligence and Security (DRS), a powerful state security service, and replaced it with officers more loyal to him.

In addition to the military, Algeria also has the National Gendarmerie, a paramilitary police force that works in rural areas. The Ministry of the Interior controls the police that work in cities.

Regional and Local Government

Algeria is divided into forty-eight provinces called *wilayas*. Each has a governor, an executive council, and an elected assembly. Governors are appointed by the president, and each governor is responsible for all interaction between the national government and the wilaya.

Each wilaya is subdivided into administrative districts and communes. These levels of government handle local concerns.

Algeria's Capital City

Algiers, the capital of Algeria and its largest city, has about 2.3 million residents. It is the economic and cultural center of the nation.

The city is nicknamed Algiers the White because many of its many gleaming white buildings are set off by the blue of the Mediterranean Sea. Algiers has long been an important harbor, with a seafaring history that reaches back to the Phoenicians in the 1100s BCE.

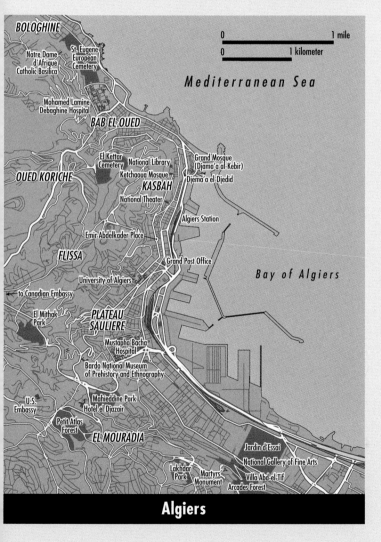

Algiers

BOLOGHINE
Notre Dame d'Afrique Catholic Basilica
St. Eugene European Cemetery
Mediterranean Sea
0 — 1 mile
0 — 1 kilometer
Mohamed Lamine Debaghine Hospital
BAB EL OUED
El Kettar Cemetery
National Library
Ketchaoua Mosque
Grand Mosque (Djama'a al-Kebir)
Djema'a el-Djedid
OUED KORICHE
KASBAH
National Theater
Algiers Station
Emir Abdelkader Place
FLISSA
Grand Post Office
University of Algiers
Bay of Algiers
to Canadian Embassy
El Mithak Park
PLATEAU SAULIERE
Mustapha Bacha Hospital
Bardo National Museum of Prehistory and Ethnography
U.S. Embassy
Mahieddine Park
Hotel el Djazair
Petit Atlas Forest
EL MOURADIA
Jardin d'Essai
National Gallery of Fine Arts
Lakhdar Park
Martyrs Monument
Villa Abd-el-Tif
Arcades Forest

Thousands of people live in the oldest part of the city, the Kasbah. This jumble of homes, warehouses, shops, and alleys also draws many tourists. The city has many fine French colonial buildings. One of the most notable sites in the city is the 330-foot-tall (100 m) Martyrs' Monument (above), which commemorates the Algerian war for independence.

CHAPTER 6

It's the Oil

ALGERIA'S MAIN INDUSTRY IS THE PUMPING and refining of oil and gas products. The oil industry accounts for more than 95 percent of Algeria's export revenues. Money earned from oil contributes two-thirds of the country's budget.

Oil and Gas

Oil was first discovered in Algeria in 1956, in the Hassi Messaoud fields in the central part of the country. The oil sector quickly became Algeria's economic mainstay, as worldwide demand for oil soared. By 1989, Algeria's five oil refineries were churning out 470,000 barrels per day. The largest refinery,

Opposite: **Algerian workers on an oil rig in Hassi Messaoud, the nation's first productive oil field**

An oil rig in Hassi Messaoud in 1959. Most of the oil in Algeria has been found in remote regions.

Skikda, is located along Algeria's northern coastline and is the biggest in Africa. Algeria's largest natural gas field, Hassi R'Mel, was also discovered in 1956. It accounts for about three-fifths of the nation's natural gas production.

Algeria has an estimated twelve billion barrels of oil reserves and produces about 1.2 million barrels a day. (An oil barrel [abbreviated as bbl] is a unit of volume equal to 42 gallons [159 liters].) Algeria is also Africa's largest producer of natural gas and has the tenth-largest natural gas reserves in the world.

Watching Over the Business

The state-run Sonatrach Group oversees all oil and gas projects in Algeria. The country has many foreign investment partners that help finance production and provide skilled workers. Among the outside firms are CEPSA and Repsol from Spain, BP from the United Kingdom, Eni from Italy, Total from France, Statoil from Norway, and Anadarko from the United States. In 2010, the Algerian government initiated a policy concerning foreign investment in the country. It gives the government majority ownership—at least a 51 percent share—in the operations of outside companies. It also gives Algeria a seat on each company's board of directors.

Algeria exported more than 1.7 trillion cubic feet of natural gas in 2012, of which approximately 1.2 trillion cubic feet was shipped through pipelines and the remainder by tanker truck. More than 90 percent of Algeria's pipeline exports are sent to Italy, Spain, and other European countries.

Signs of the oil and gas industry are everywhere in Algeria. In the harsh desert where the drilling occurs, sprawling refineries spread across the landscape. Fires from burning gas are vivid against the bright blue sky. From horizon to horizon, towering derricks rise above the wells. Storage tanks squat behind protective dikes to hold back leaks. A spiderweb of pipelines connect the fields with the refineries and seaport terminals. Wearing dark safety glasses and clamping protective hard hats low over their foreheads, hundreds of workers toil under the hot sun in the oil fields and at the refineries. They ensure that the oil and gas keep flowing.

Remote fields make tempting targets for militants, however. In January 2013, terrorists attacked the Amenas gas facility in southern Algeria near the Libyan border. They took hundreds of hostages and murdered forty workers from several countries, including the United States. As Algerian forces tried to capture the militants, the facility was heavily damaged. Security has been increased at facilities around the country, but militants continue trying to attack. In 2016, there were rocket attacks on

Algerian workers construct a pipeline used to bring natural gas to Europe.

The Struggle to Find Work

Until Algeria gained independence in 1962, its economy was primarily based on agriculture. France was its major trading partner. With the discovery of oil, farming declined in importance, and many people moved to the cities to seek well-paying jobs. But many Algerians still struggle to find work. Some young people become street peddlers. Many can find nothing but short-term jobs. High unemployment and a lack of job opportunities have been the root causes of social unrest in Algeria.

oil refineries, but no one was hurt. Any disruption in the flow of Algerian oil and gas would cause shortages and affect prices, especially in Europe.

Mining

Since ancient times, valuable minerals and stone have been dug up in North Africa. During the Roman occupation of Numidia, in what is now Algeria, slaves labored in at least three hundred quarries, cutting precious marble for use in Roman temples and other public buildings. Remains of these deep pits can be toured near Kléber. Beautifully translucent onyx was dug up at Ain Tekbaleli, near Tlemcen.

Today, Algeria mines iron, gold, and silver, and many industrial materials such as barite, dolomite, and feldspar. Marble is still dug from the ground. Algeria provides 2 percent of the world's pumice and 1 percent of its gypsum. Phosphate

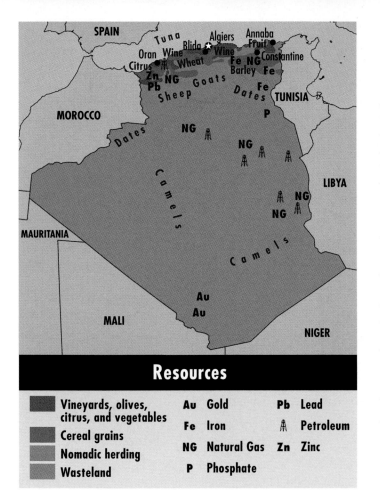

Resources

▮ Vineyards, olives, citrus, and vegetables	Au	Gold	Pb	Lead
▮ Cereal grains	Fe	Iron	⛏	Petroleum
▮ Nomadic herding	NG	Natural Gas	Zn	Zinc
▮ Wasteland	P	Phosphate		

has been mined since 1891. Salt found at the edges of chotts is in high demand.

Manufacturing

Algerian industries are concentrated around Algiers and Oran. The country's factories include carpet mills, automobile assembly facilities, and food-processing facilities. Algerian companies also produce bricks and tiles, farm machinery, electrical supplies, machine tools, phosphates, sulfuric acid, paper and cartons, matches, and soap.

Algeria has a small but growing steel industry. The country's only production facility is the El Hadjar complex in the northeast, which can produce about 2 million tons of steel a year. Cement is another growth industry, with Algeria's twelve plants putting out about 11.5 million tons a year.

Agriculture and Fishing

About 11 percent of Algerian workers are employed in agriculture. The three primary crops grown in Algeria are potatoes, wheat, and barley. Other major Algerian products are dates, cork, and tobacco.

Olive trees also contribute to Algeria's economy. Some of the olives are eaten. Others are pressed to make olive oil. Algeria is among the top twenty-five olive-producing countries in the world. With full sun, well-drained sandy soil, water, and a long, hot growing season, olive trees need little care and can live five hundred years. Nectarines, oranges, figs, apricots, and almonds are also grown on Algerian farms.

Despite the many fruits and vegetables grown within their own country, the people of Algeria need much more food than they can produce. Consequently, about 45 percent of the food in Algeria is imported.

A farmer harvests huge bunches of dates from high in a date palm tree. Each bunch can contain as many as one thousand dates.

Herders bring sheep to a market in the M'zab Valley in central Algeria. Raising sheep is an important part of the economy in rural areas.

For centuries, nomads in what is now Algeria moved their flocks from pasture to pasture so they could graze. In modern times, this practice has mostly faded away. Today, sheep are the most common livestock in Algeria, accounting for about 80 percent of the animals. Sheep are a major source of meat, wool, and milk. The second most common agricultural animals in Algeria are goats, accounting for 13 percent of Algeria's animals. A few milk cows are raised in the north of the country.

Fish farming has become a growing industry in recent years. Working with South Korean investors, Algeria launched two shrimp-farming projects in seawater and one in a freshwater facility. More traditionally, fishers cast their nets in Algeria's

Mediterranean waters for catches to be either consumed by the home market or exported. Among the commercial species are sole, sea bass, tilapia, eel, swordfish, and sardines. Algeria also imports frozen tuna, hake, and other kinds of fish from Spain, India, and China.

What Algeria Grows, Makes, and Mines

AGRICULTURE

Potatoes (2012)	4,219,476 metric tons
Wheat (2012)	3,432,231 metric tons
Sheep (2013)	25,500,000 animals

MANUFACTURING (VALUE OF EXPORTS, 2014)

Refined petroleum	$12,700,000,000
Food products	$289,000,000
Machinery	$54,500,000

MINING

Oil (2015)	1,157,100,000 barrels per day
Natural gas (2013)	79,650,000,000 cubic meters
Gold (2015)	174 metric tons

Communications

More than thirty million Algerians, or about three-quarters of the population, use the Internet. Young Algerians are savvy users of social media. In 2011, antigovernment demonstrators organized rallies using social media. This prompted the government to block access to some Web sites and news agencies.

A man reads a newspaper at a stand in Algiers.

The restrictions were eventually loosened, but they demonstrated that the Algerian government will limit what can be expressed publicly.

Access to news is prized by ordinary Algerians. The country has more than forty-five major newspapers, publish-

Algerian Currency

The basic unit of Algerian money is the dinar. There are coins worth 5, 10, 20, 50, and 100 dinars. In 2012, a special 200-dinar coin was issued to mark the fiftieth anniversary of Algerian independence. There are also 200, 500, and 1,000 dinar banknotes. In 2016, 109 dinars equaled US$1.

The banknotes are beautifully illustrated, depicting important images from Algerian history and culture, with subjects ranging from cave paintings to battle scenes to scientists working in a laboratory.

ing in Arabic, French, Tamazight, and English. The largest Arabic-language publications include the independent tabloid *Echourouk* and the pro-government *El Massa*. French-language newspapers include *El Watan* and the government-owned *El Moudjahid*. The Algérie Presse Service is the national press agency. While there is no official press censorship, editors and reporters can get into trouble by speaking out on corruption and other issues that might upset the government.

Satellite broadcasts of French and Arab television stations are popular, with an estimated thirty-four million satellite dishes around the country. ENTV is the state-owned TV station, and Dzair TV is privately owned. Radio Algérienne is the public radio broadcasting company. Many radio stations also stream over the Internet.

An Algerian man reads the Internet.

Transportation

Algeria's varied terrain presents transportation challenges. Nobody wants to break down in an endless expanse of sun-scorched sand and rock while crossing the desert. Algeria has two routes in the Trans-African Highway network. One is the well-used north–south Trans-Sahara Highway. Construction on the other, an east–west freeway all the way across Algeria, began in 2007. This six-lane highway is 756 miles (1,217 km) long and is considered one of the world's largest public works projects.

There are 2,469 miles (3,973 km) of railway in Algeria. Two

Camels cross a road, stopping traffic in the middle of the Sahara Desert.

high-speed passenger routes operate between Algiers, Oran, Annaba, and Constantine. Many passengers also use a central bus terminal on the outskirts of downtown Algiers, where they can catch rides to cities such as Oran, Ouargla, and Annaba.

A faster way to travel is to fly Air Algérie to many locations around the country. The nation's main international airport, Houari Boumediene Airport, is about 12 miles (20 km) southeast of the capital. Turkish Airlines, Air France, Lufthansa, Royal Jordanian, and British Airways are some of the busiest airlines serving Algeria.

Algeria also has a number of modern ports where large ships from around the world load and unload cargo. The largest ports are in Algiers and Oran.

Changing Economy

In the two decades after becoming independent, Algeria had a socialist government that emphasized a centrally planned economy. Major industries such as oil were nationalized and multiyear economic plans were put into practice. These limits were gradually eased during the 1980s. In 1994, the privatization of some state-owned businesses was allowed. Many small firms are now privately owned. The country is working hard to improve its economy by constructing research centers, improving its transportation system, and building better quality housing.

With its reserves of minerals, gas, and oil; its ever-expanding industrial capacity; and an eager workforce, Algeria's economy has much potential.

CHAPTER 7

The Algerian People

I N 2016, ALGERIA'S POPULATION REACHED 40,407,913, making it the thirty-third largest country in the world. Nearly a third of the population was under age fifteen. Men in Algeria can expect to live seventy-six years, while women typically live seventy-eight years.

About 90 percent of the population lives in the fertile Tell, avoiding the sand and rock that covers most of the country. Some 70 percent of the people make their homes in the larger cities where most of the job opportunities are. Many Algerians moved to the city from rural areas in search of work and now live in slums surrounding the capital.

Opposite: **Young boys in Algiers**

Population of Largest Cities	
Algiers	2,364,230
Oran	893,329
Constantine	448,028
Annaba	342,793
Blida	331,779

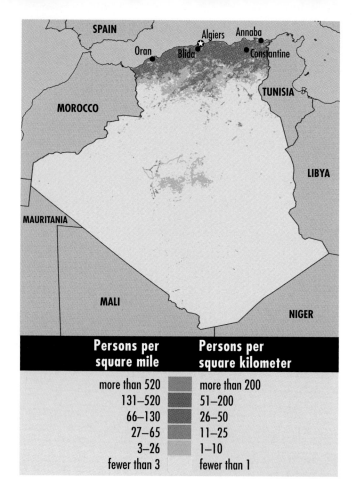

Persons per square mile		Persons per square kilometer
more than 520		more than 200
131–520		51–200
66–130		26–50
27–65		11–25
3–26		1–10
fewer than 3		fewer than 1

Berber and Arab

The Berbers were the first people to settle permanently in what is now Algeria, several thousand years ago. Arabs arrived in the seventh century CE, bringing Islam with them. Most Berbers soon converted to Islam.

The new religion transformed their cultural and social identity. Over the generations, Arabs and Berbers intermarried. Most people in Algeria today are a mix of Berber and Arab ethnicities. But some Berber groups retain a separate identity.

Berbers gather for a funeral in Ghardaïa.

Tuareg

The Tuareg are a Berber people who have lived in the Sahara for thousands of years. Their ability to adapt to the desert's often deadly living conditions is an indication of their strength and resilience. *Tuareg* is an Arabic term meaning "abandoned by God." But these proud men and women prefer to call themselves Imohag, meaning "free men."

When they are considered adults, many young Tuareg men wear blue veils over their faces to shield them from the sand and sun. The wrappings indicate they are of marriageable age. The indigo dye in the turbans can stain their skin, so the Tuareg are sometimes nicknamed the Blue Men of the

Tuareg men often cover their faces while Tuareg women do not.

Desert. Unlike Tuareg men. Tuareg women do not wear the blue veils. Instead, they use different wrappings as protective headgear. Today, there are an estimated one to two million Tuareg spread across North Africa.

In ancient times, the Tuareg controlled the major trade routes across the desert. They sometimes demanded payment from merchant caravans for safe passage. The Tuareg themselves were also great traders, transporting beads, flour, ceramics, salt, saffron, dates, and other goods from the coast to central Africa. They returned north with slaves and gold.

Tuareg women return home from the market in Timimoun, a desert city in central Algeria.

Many Tuareg also grew crops and were skilled herders, moving goats, camels, and horses from oasis to oasis. In 1916, a Tuareg rebellion against the French was crushed and their nomadic ways slowly began disappearing. By the twenty-first century, borders between countries made it more difficult for the Tuareg to live a nomadic lifestyle. Drought also affected Tuareg livestock breeding and dried up their crops. The shortage of pastureland and water prompted most Tuareg to settle in towns. Many now drive trucks rather than ride camels or herd goats.

Although most Algerians now use trucks to cross the desert, some people still travel using camels and donkeys.

Ethnic Population	
Arab or Arab-Berber mix	83%
Berber	16%
European	1%

Men hold their weapons high during a fantasia demonstration.

Other Berber Groups

The Kabyle are another subgroup of the Berber people. Their homeland in the rugged Aurès Mountains has protected them from the region's many invaders over the generations. The towering peaks and deep valleys of this mountain range provided cover for Algerian rebels during the revolt against the French in the 1950s and 1960s.

The Berber ethnic group called the Chaouia are noted horsemen who perform an elaborate display of skill called a fantasia at festivals and weddings. During a fantasia, armed riders charge straight ahead at the same time and fire their guns into the sky at the end of the run. The gunfire is timed so precisely that it sounds like a single blast.

The M'zab people have lived along a plateau in the southern Sahara since the eleventh century. They built five walled cities called *ksour*. The M'zab cities are very well designed, with tightly packed buildings separated by narrow passageways. Three thousand wells support the M'zab towns, which are known for their abundant palm trees.

Europeans

About a million Europeans once lived in Algeria. Most were of French heritage. After Algeria gained its independence from France, more than 90 percent of the Europeans departed.

In the ancient cities of the M'zab Valley, buildings are constructed in concentric circles around a mosque.

Today, only 1 percent of Algeria's population is of European descent. Most have ancestry in Mediterranean countries such as France, Italy, and Spain.

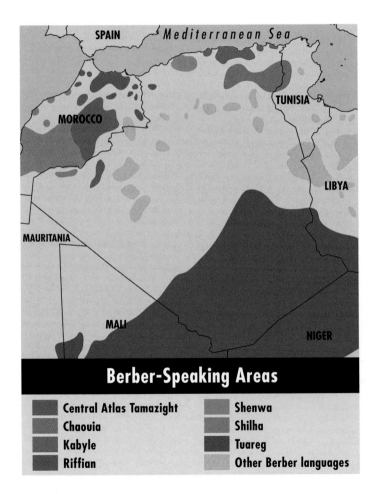

Berber-Speaking Areas

- Central Atlas Tamazight
- Chaouia
- Kabyle
- Riffian
- Shenwa
- Shilha
- Tuareg
- Other Berber languages

Languages

Arabic is the most common language in Algeria, spoken at home by more than 70 percent of the population. Arabic is the sacred language of Islam, spoken throughout North Africa and the Middle East. Arabic is written from right to left using beautiful, curving lines. English words such as *zero*, *syrup*, *adobe*, *coffee*, and *algebra* are all derived from the Arabic language.

Algeria has two official languages, Arabic and the Berber language of Tamazight. After independence, Arabic was preferred, and for years, Berbers sought to have their language taught in schools. In 2002, it was finally recognized as a national, but not an official, language. This allowed it to be taught as a second language in Berber areas. But the Berbers hoped for more, holding strikes and protests to gain recognition of Tamazight. Finally, in 2016, their language was fully recognized by the government. There are many different varieties of the Berber language, including Kabyle and Tuareg.

Most Algerians also speak French. In addition, English is frequently used for international business dealings.

Education

Before Algeria became independent, children of French heritage received the best teachers and classrooms while schools for Arabs and Berbers struggled. In 1949, segregation in the school system was prohibited. Yet as late as 1958, only 12 percent of Algerian children attended school, and few Muslim

Arabic is written in an elegant script that reads from right to left on the page.

youngsters continued beyond primary grades. Religious scholars in the Association of Algerian Muslim Ulama and other Arab education advocates lobbied hard for equal educational opportunities. Eventually, their efforts paid off.

Today, education is mandatory and free for all Algerian children through nine years of primary school. A typical school day lasts six hours. Lessons are taught in Arabic throughout the country, and in Tamazight in Berber areas. Children study history, science, and the arts. Classes include writing in Arabic calligraphy, a highly prized skill. Western-style writing is also taught.

Fewer than half the children who complete primary school continue on to secondary education. Sometimes, their parents do not encourage further schooling because they want their children to help provide for the family.

Secondary school lasts three years in Algeria. Young people who would rather learn trades can attend vocational school, which lasts from one to four years.

If young people want to go to college, they must pass a test. In 2016, Algeria had sixty-four institutions of higher education. Most are in Algiers, Oran, and Constantine. The oldest college in the nation is the University of Algiers, founded in 1909. It offers degrees in law, medicine, pharmacy, sciences, and other specialties. Most courses are taught in Arabic or French, but English is often used in science and medical classes.

With the oil economy predominant in Algeria, schools such as the University of Sciences and Technology offer excellent studies in geology, math, and other sciences important to that industry. The Ministry of Energy and Mines and the Ministry of Agriculture and Rural Development also have several institutes. Approximately one million Algerian students are enrolled in these centers, along with about eighty thousand international students. Many students move on to government or judicial positions upon graduation.

CHAPTER 8

No God but God

ISLAM IS THE OFFICIAL RELIGION IN ALGERIA, practiced by most of the country's residents. It permeates every aspect of life, and its principles provide a strong base for the country's ethics.

Opposite: **Women read the Qur'an at a mosque in Algiers.**

Before Islam

People lived in the region that is now Algeria long before Islam arose. Thousands of years ago, North Africans were pagans, worshipping many different gods. Some Berbers in the mountainous interior adopted Judaism. On the coast, many people became Christian during the Roman occupation.

Among the early Christian leaders was Saint Augustine (354–430 CE). He was bishop of Hippo, now the Algerian city of Annaba. His mother, Saint Monica, was a Berber who converted to Christianity and encouraged her son's religious studies. Other noted Christian leaders from the region were Origen and Clement of Alexandria, and Tertullian and Cyprian of Carthage.

The Muslim Way

Like Judaism and Christianity, Islam is monotheistic, meaning it follows only one God. The Arabic word *Islam* means "submission to the will of God." The Arabic word for God is *Allah*.

Muslims believe that everyone is created equal in the sight of God. Islam also recognizes that all humans make mistakes and sin, so peace and mercy are important. Justice, tolerance, equality, and love are also important values. According to Islam, a person should con-

Saint Augustine was one of the most important philosophers in early Christianity.

Muhammad, Islam's major religious figure, was born around the year 570 CE in what is now the Saudi Arabian city of Mecca. He disliked many of the religious practices of the time and journeyed into the desert to pray and reflect. Muslims believe that the angel Gabriel appeared to Muhammad in 610 and told him to proclaim God's message. It is said that Gabriel returned to Muhammad many times in the following years, bringing many more messages from God. These thoughts were written down, becoming the Qur'an.

Although Muhammad was persecuted for his religious beliefs, he began attracting followers. He eventually fled to a city called Medina, where he expanded his influence. Muhammad became the most important and revered figure in the Arab world. Within one hundred years of his death in 632, Islam had spread to many parts of the world.

duct himself or herself in a manner that does not hurt others. Women are respected under Islam and are considered equal to men because they are all God's creation.

Islam is based on revelations that the Prophet Muhammad is said to have received from God. These revelations are collected in the Islamic holy book, the Qur'an.

Judaism, Christianity, and Islam all stem from the same spiritual roots. Figures such as Adam, Moses, Jesus, and John the Baptist appear in the Qur'an. Muslims consider them powerful prophets. Other important Islamic traditions stem from the sayings and actions of Muhammad and his companions. These are collected in a text called the Hadith.

The Five Pillars of Islam

- Muslims must repeat the declaration of faith: There is no god but God, and Muhammad is the messenger of God.
- Muslims must pray five times a day, facing Mecca.
- Muslims must give alms, or donations, to the needy.
- Muslims must refrain from eating and drinking between dawn and sundown in the month of Ramadan as a means of purification.
- Muslims must make a pilgrimage to Mecca once in their lifetime if they are physically and financially able to.

The two main branches of Islam are Sunni and Shia. Almost all Muslims in Algeria belong to the Sunni branch. Some Berbers also practice a form of Islam called Sufism. Others revere Muslim holy men called marabouts who offered their own pathways to salvation.

Islamic law outlines the disciplines and principles governing a Muslim's behavior. Among the rules, Muslims are not supposed to eat pork, drink alcohol, or gamble.

At the Mosque

It is the duty of every Muslim to pray five times each day: at dawn, noon, afternoon, sunset, and night. Clergy called muezzin announce when it is time to pray from a minaret, a tall tower at a mosque. Today at most mosques the call to prayer is broadcast through loudspeakers atop a minaret.

Call to Prayer

The same call to prayer is given at mosques around the world:

Allahu Akbar, Allahu Akbar	God is the greatest, God is the greatest.
Allahu Akbar, Allahu Akbar	God is the greatest, God is the greatest.
Ashadu an la ilaha ill Allah	I bear witness that there is none worthy of worship but God.
Ashadu an la ilaha ill Allah	I bear witness that there is none worthy of worship but God.
Ashadu anna Muhammadan rasoolullah	I bear witness that Muhammad is the prophet of God.
Ashadu anna Muhammadan rasoolullah	I bear witness that Muhammad is the prophet of God.
Hayya'alas salah	Come to prayer.
Hayya'alas salah	Come to prayer.
Hayya'alal falah	Come to success.
Hayya'alal falah	Come to success.
Allahu Akbar, Allahu Akbar	God is the greatest, God is the greatest.
La ilaha ill Allah	There is no god but God.

Near the Bay of Algiers, the world's tallest minaret was completed at the Djamaa El Djazair mosque in 2016. At 870 feet (265 m), it soars above the capital's skyline. Other beautiful mosques in Algiers include the Djama'a al-Kebir, the Great Mosque, constructed in 1097, and the Djema'a el-Djedid, built by the Turks in 1660.

When entering a mosque, worshippers take off their shoes and kneel on prayer rugs. A mosque is considered the best place to pray, but Muslims can pray anywhere.

Muslim Holidays

The Islamic calendar is lunar, meaning it is aligned with the patterns of the moon. This lunar calendar is eleven days shorter than the Western calendar, so Islamic holidays do not fall on the same date from one year to the next.

Sacred Sites

Algiers is the spiritual as well as the political capital of Algeria, but other cities around the country are also noted holy locales. Tlemcen, in northwest Algeria, has more buildings dating from the twelfth to the fifteenth centuries than any other Algerian community. The Great Mosque, built in 1136, is a well-known landmark. Many of the city's early rulers are buried in the courtyard of Sidi Bel Hassan Mosque, dating from 1296. Other prominent sites include the Mosque of Sidi Boumediene, from about 1328, and the Synagogue of Tlemcen, from about 1392. Tlemcen fell into decline at the end of the fourteenth century and was overpowered by the Turks in 1559.

Al-Hijra, the Islamic New Year, is celebrated on the first day of Muharram, the month in which Muhammad moved from Mecca to Medina in 622 CE. According to tradition, if people spend a lot of money on their families on the tenth of Muharram, the first month of the year, they will be blessed by God throughout the year.

Ramadan is the ninth month of the Muslim year. In daylight hours during Ramadan, Muslims take part in a fast, meaning they do not eat or drink. Many spend time in prayer. Pregnant women, children, the sick, and the elderly do not have to fast during Ramadan. At sunset, everyone sits down for a delicious dinner. Laylat al-Qadr, the "Night of Power," is a special day near the end of Ramadan. It is said to be the day Muhammad received his first revelation from the angel Gabriel.

Eid al-Fitr is another of Islam's major festivals. It is the joyful end of Ramadan, celebrated over three days. During this time, people often visit friends and relatives.

Eid al-Adha, the Festival of the Sacrifice, is observed at the conclusion of the hajj, the pilgrimage to Mecca. During this festival, every family that can afford to sacrifices something, usually a sheep. The meat from the sheep is shared. The family gives one-third of the meat to the poor and one-third to neighbors and keeps one-third for themselves. True to Islam's emphasis on charity, no one is left out.

Mawlid an-Nabi marks the birthday of Muhammad. Gala processions, poetry readings, festive singing, drumming, and the giving of balloons to children are all part of the fun.

Abdelhamid Ben Badis: Muslim Leader

Abdelhamid Ben Badis (1889–1940) was the dynamic leader of the Islamic reform movement in Algeria. In 1931, he organized the Association of Algerian Muslim Ulama, encouraging his country's Islamic scholars to come together despite their opposing viewpoints. *Ulama* is Arabic for "the learned ones."

Ben Badis had grown up in a religious household that valued education. By the age of thirteen, he had memorized the entire Qur'an and went on to university to learn more about his faith. He realized that some elements of Islam could be updated, a view opposed by some clergy who did not see the need for reform. Ben Badis became a teacher at the Sidi Qammouch mosque in Constantine.

He also became involved in politics. He was strongly nationalistic and believed that a free Algeria should be Arab and Muslim.

Many Algerians visit the graves of their relatives during Eid al-Fitr.

Religious Freedom

Algeria's constitution guarantees freedom of religion. There are some restrictions, though. For example, it is illegal to try to convert people to other religions. Most non-Muslims, however, are able to practice their religion in peace.

Estimates of the number of Christian and Jewish citizens in Algeria vary from fifty thousand to one hundred thousand. The number of Jewish people in Algeria has declined significantly in recent decades, as many people left the country amid the upheaval and violence. In 2014, the government promised to reopen twenty-five synagogues that were shuttered during the turmoil, but by 2016, only a few were open because of the lack of worshippers.

Because of its French heritage, Algeria's largest Christian denomination is Roman Catholicism, the most common religion in France. During French rule, there were more than one million Roman Catholics in Algeria. After independence, the numbers declined as thousands fled to Europe. In 2007, government officials attended a ceremony at the Notre Dame d'Afrique Catholic basilica in Algiers to celebrate the completion of a three-year renovation project. The church had originally been built in the 1870s as a symbol of tolerance.

A Jewish cemetery in Ghardaïa. Many Algerian cities once had significant Jewish populations.

The phrase "Our Lady of Africa, pray for us and the Muslims" is inscribed over the altar.

Protestants such as Anglicans and Seventh-day Adventists are allowed to hold services as long as they don't interfere with the practice of Islam.

Religion and Government

Since the founding of independent Algeria, the government has controlled all religious practices. The Ministry of

Protestant Berber women attend a service in the city of Tizi Ouzou. In Algeria, it is illegal to try to convert Muslims to another religion.

Religious Affairs provides financial support to mosques and pays the salaries of imams, Islamic worship leaders and preachers. The state also hires and trains imams. Muslim religious services, except for daily prayers, can be performed only in state-sanctioned mosques. The ministry ensures that pupils have religious education, keeps track of how the media reports on religious affairs, and makes certain that Algerians keep the Ramadan fast.

An imam speaks at a mosque in Algiers.

CHAPTER 9

It's All in the Art

ALGERIA'S LONG HISTORY OF CONQUEST, colonization, and drive for independence has been fertile ground for creativity. The country's painters, sculptors, writers, filmmakers, designers, poets, and other artists produce internationally respected masterpieces. The Algerian people are proud of this explosion of invention.

Opposite: **Traditional musicians perform at a wedding in the Sahara.**

Visual Arts

Algerian art has had a storied history, encompassing ancient cave paintings, Roman ruins, mosques with elaborate mosaics, grand Turkish palaces, and ornate European-style buildings.

Glass bottles dating back to the seventh century BCE have been discovered in Constantine. They are now on display at the Cirta National Museum.

Several Algerian museums showcase artifacts from these many cultures. The Cirta National Museum in Constantine opened in 1931. Its fine arts wing exhibits paintings and sculptures with Algerian themes produced between the seventeenth and twentieth centuries. The Museum of Modern and Contemporary Art in Algiers opened to much fanfare in 2007 with a show by contemporary Algerian painter Malek Saleh. Since then, it has hosted many major exhibitions. The National Gallery of Fine Arts in Algiers is another attractive facility. It has showcased artists such as Ferdinand Victor Eugène Delacroix, Mohammed Racim, and Nasreddine Dinet.

There are many rising stars in the art world in Algeria. One of the best known is Oussama Tabti, who graduated from the Academy of Fine Arts in Algiers in 2012. Using video, found objects, and drawings, he delves into North African, colonial, and post-colonial themes.

Visual artist Patrick Altes was born in Algeria and is of French and Spanish ancestry. Through his art, he tries to encourage dialogue between North Africans and Europeans. He combines his own images with antique photographs taken both by French settlers and Arab Algerians, connecting the cultures.

The building that houses the Museum of Modern and Contemporary Art in Algiers was constructed in the early twentieth century as a department store.

Kader Attia grew up in Algeria and Paris. His dynamic art pieces explore the experience of living within two cultures. One installation called *Arab Spring* features shattered display cases and broken glass and rocks, evoking images of looted museums.

During the French colonial regime, local culture was largely suppressed while French styles were encouraged. But since independence, the government has supported Berber, Arab, and Islamic culture. Handicraft centers have been funded, encouraging traditional arts such as rug weaving, brass work, pottery, and jewelry design.

A training center in the Berber town of Khenchela offers classes in carpet weaving. Traditional Berber carpets can take three months to make.

Music

Some contemporary Algerian composers incorporate traditional instruments into their music. These include the *oud*, a stringed instrument similar to the lute, and the *rhita*, or reed flute. Some traditional Algerian music also includes storytelling. Men wear long white robes, called *jellahas*, and sing lyrical tales of romance, bravery, and family.

Many different kinds of music flourish in Algeria today. Andalus classical arrived in North Africa from Spain in the seventeenth century. Poetic *chaabi* originated in Algiers. It

An Algerian musician plays an oud. Some ouds have ten strings, while others have eleven or thirteen.

A wide variety of music is popular in Algeria. Singer and guitarist Souad Massi plays music that mixes rock with more traditional Algerian music.

is wistful music, telling the story of lost love. Raï is an infectious blend of Arab, African, and Western music. It rose out of the street music of Oran, becoming popular through Cheb Khaled's songs. Berber music from the Kabyle, which has nationalistic overtones, remains popular. Two well-known opera stars are tenor Mahieddine Bachtarzi and Berber-French soprano Amel Brahim-Djelloul. The Oran-born violinist and singer Akim el Sikameya combines jazz, flamenco, gypsy, and traditional Algerian music in his unique presentations.

From Oran to the World

The politically charged folk music raï (pronounced "RYE") originated in Oran. *Raï* means "opinion" in Arabic. The style is rooted in shepherds' songs from the early 1900s, but it also includes elements of Western music. Young raï musicians call themselves *cheb* while older performers are *sheikh*. Noted performers Cheb Hasni, Cheb Khaled (right), and Rachid Taha came from Oran.

Conservative Algerians have sometimes objected to raï because it deals with social issues. They have also objected because women, called *cheikhas*, sing in public in front of men. In 1988, the government blamed raï for the unrest that swept Algeria as people demanded economic reforms. Despite efforts to censor it, raï remained popular. In the 1990s, extremists continued to object to the music, however, and they assassinated several raï singers, including Cheb Hasni, because the singers rejected radicalism.

Cheb Khaled's "El Harba Wayn" ("To Flee, But Where?") remains one of the genre's most popular tunes. Its lyrics include:

Where has youth gone?
Where are the brave ones?
The rich gorge themselves
The poor work themselves to death
The Islamic charlatans show their true face . . .
You can always cry or complain
Or escape . . . but where?

Algerians love rock music. Fella Ababsa, who also goes by the name Fulla, is signed with Rotana, the biggest record company in the Middle East. Popular R & B singer Zehira Darabid, known as Zaho, was born in Oran and moved to Montreal, Canada, when she was eighteen. The Dar K' Side rockers call Oran their hometown. They have toured the United States, revving up crowds wherever they appeared. Hip-hop and rap also have fans in Algeria, with popular acts including Intik, Raouf Adear, and Rim'K.

The Danger of Art

Algerian artists must often be careful, especially if dealing with political or religious themes in their work. Extreme conservative groups sometimes target them for their views. A major exhibit in the United Arab Emirates by Algerian writer and visual artist Mustapha Benfodil was taken down in 2011. It was considered too provocative because it gave voice to victims assaulted by religious extremists.

Some artists and writers have been assassinated for expressing their viewpoints. More than 150 journalists were killed during Algeria's civil war of the 1990s. Among them were Mustafa Abada, the director of Algerian state television, and writer Tahar Djaout (right), whose final manuscript, *The Last Summer of Reason*, told of a bookseller's battle against extremists. Singer Lounès Matoub (below) was killed by terrorists in 1998. Of Berber heritage, Matoub was

highly respected for his pro-democracy views and for opposing militant Islamists. Matoub had cofounded the Algerian Human Rights League and sang protest songs in cafés and bars. One of his famous albums was *Ay Izem* (*The Lion*). Others killed include raï record producer Rachid Baba Ahmed; singer Cheb Aziz; poet Youcef Sebti; actor Azzedine Medjoubi; Abdelkader Alloula, manager of the National Theater; and Ahmed Asselah, president of the Algiers School of Fine Arts.

In the 2000s, the terrorism quieted, allowing Algerian arts to flourish again. Galleries opened, poetry readings were held, and lively concerts attracted music fans.

Film

Moviemaking has a long history in North Africa. News shorts were shot in the region as far back as 1909. During the silent film era of the 1920s, many films were shot in Algeria, including *L'Atlantide*, one of the earliest films about the French colonial experience in North Africa. After independence, Algerian films won praise, particularly for dramas and documentaries dealing with social issues, colonialism, and revolution.

Algerian director Mohammed Lakhdar-Hamina is one of the most notable figures in contemporary Arab cinema. His 1966 film *The Winds of the Aures* received the Best First Work Award at the prestigious Cannes Film Festival in France. One of the most renowned films of this era is *The Battle of Algiers*, an Algerian-Italian film that earned three Academy Award

A scene from *The Battle of Algiers*, a passionate film about the Algerian fight for independence. It is considered one of the greatest political films of all time.

nominations. Edited to look like a documentary, it showed the Algerian struggle for independence.

Other Algerian films include Mohamed Oukassi's 1994 comedy *Carnaval fi Dachra*. It tells of a poor farmer who runs for mayor of his town and then dreams of being the country's president. Merzak Allouache has directed many films, including *The Repentant*, which was acclaimed at the 2012 Cannes Film Festival. *The Algerian* is a political thriller from 2014 starring Algiers-born actor Ben Youcef.

Literature

Authors are highly respected in Algeria for their creativity and storytelling abilities. Each year, the Algiers International Book Fair attracts thousands of people from around the world. The event celebrated its twentieth year in 2015 with fifty-three countries represented.

One of the earliest known writers from what is now Algeria was Lucius Apuleius (ca. 124–170? CE), a Roman philosopher born in the ancient kingdom of Numidia. His works include the humorous *Golden Ass*, considered one of the world's first novels. A much more recent Algerian novelist was Albert Camus (1913–1960). He created tragic characters who muddle through absurd situations in order to survive. Both a philosopher and prolific author, Camus wrote novels, short stories, and nonfiction. His best-known books are *The Stranger* and *The Plague*. Camus received the Nobel Prize in Literature, the world's greatest literary honor, in 1957.

Kateb Yacine (1929–1989) was another influential

Algerian writer. His critically acclaimed *Nedjma*, published in 1956, was set during the Algerian revolution against the French. Yacine was a fervent nationalist, and his main character was said to represent Algeria itself.

Well-known Berber writers include Mouloud Mammeri (1917–1989) and Mouloud Feraoun (1913–1962), who was assassinated by the French.

Assia Djebar (1936–2015) was a novelist and filmmaker who studied the lives of Algerian women in her books *So Vast the Prison* and *A Sister to Scheherazade*. She was born Fatima-Zohra Imalayen, but adopted her pen name. Also using a pen name was Mohammed Moulessehoul. An officer in the Algerian army, he used the female pen name Yasmina Khadra to avoid army censorship. In his award-winning novels, Moulessehoul describes the horrors of the 1990s civil war and the attraction of radicalism to people without power.

Albert Camus was just forty-four years old when he was awarded the Nobel Prize in Literature. He was the second-youngest person ever to be given the honor.

Soccer is the most popular sport in Algeria.

Sports

Sports are central to Algerian life. Soccer is the most popular sport in the country. Kids of all ages play the game everywhere, from empty lots to green fields. They dream of being the next Lakhdar Belloumi, a retired midfielder still considered the best Algerian player of all time. He played in many championships and then managed several Algerian teams.

Everybody goes wild when powerful players such as El Arbi Hillel Soudani and Djamel Mesbah take the field. They, like many of Algeria's greatest players, often move from club to club and country to country. Matteo Ferrari was born in Algeria and was a defender with the Montreal Impact team for three years. His father was an Italian oil engineer who worked in the Algerian oil fields and his mother was from Guinea. In 2007, Hamza Aït Ouamar was voted the most promising young player in Algerian soccer. He went on to play in Finland.

Algeria first competed at the Olympic Games in 1964. In the 1992 summer games, the quietly determined runner Hassiba Boulmerka made sports history. She earned Algeria's first Olympic gold medal, winning the 1500-meter women's run. The largest Algerian sports delegation at the Olympic Games was in 2016, when sixty-five athletes participated in the summer games. They competed in sports such as running, boxing, and fencing. Runner Taoufik Makhloufi won two silver medals at the games. Four years earlier, he had brought home a gold medal.

Taoufik Makhloufi celebrates after winning a silver medal at the 2016 Olympics.

Despite its reputation for scorching heat and sand, Algeria has a major ski resort at Chréa National Park, 44 miles (70 km) south of Algiers in the Atlas Mountains. Tourists and locals alike find the snowy slopes challenging. Though few Algerians compete in snow sports, cross-country skier Mehdi-Sélim Khelifi took part in the 2010 Winter Olympics.

Most Algerians prefer to take their vacations along the coast near Algiers and Oran rather than in the snowy mountains. On the coast, they can swim, fish, enjoy the breeze, and perhaps listen to the latest soccer games on the radio.

CHAPTER 10

Food
and Fun

ALGERIANS ARE EXTREMELY HOSPITABLE, displaying values common throughout the Arab world. On special occasions, families gather for a large meal of lamb roasted over an open fire. When guests visit, children offer a bowl of perfumed water to diners so they can wash their hands before eating. In rural areas, food is traditionally eaten with the thumb, forefinger, and middle finger of the right hand. Silverware is much more common in wealthy urban areas. People typically eat seated at a low table. Meals are leisurely, allowing everyone a chance to catch up on their latest news.

Opposite: **Men sell fruits and vegetables at a market in the oasis city of Tamanrasset.**

Favorite Foods

Algerian food is a reflection of the country's long history of invasions, with each foreign culture bringing its own cuisine. The Carthaginians brought wheat and the Romans who fol-

A woman cooks spaghetti at an oasis in the Sahara. Algerian cuisine has influences from all around the world.

lowed them planted barley and other grains. Arabs added spices transported by caravan or sailing ships from the far reaches of their empire. These ranged from brilliantly colored saffron to pungent nutmeg, ginger, cloves, and fragrant cinnamon. Turks brought pastries sticky with honey, while during the colonial era, the French brought baguettes. Still other Mediterranean cultures contributed to Algeria's ever-expanding mix on the menu. Olives, oranges, plums, and peaches were brought from Spain in the 1500s. The Spanish also provided tomatoes, potatoes, zucchini, and hot peppers from their conquests in the Americas. Many Algerian dishes are not complete without plenty of paprika, cumin, and delicate marjoram. Caraway, fennel, and coriander contribute their own special tastes. Berber influence is seen in the abundance of stews at the family table, along with goat or lamb, mounds of vegetables, grains, dates, and dried fruits.

Couscous is Algeria's national dish. This is so basic to the Algerian diet that its name in Arabic, *ta'am*, translates as "food." Couscous is made of small balls of semolina wheat. It is steamed and served in an elaborately painted clay cooking pot called a tajine. Traditionally, tajine cooking was done over a bed of hot coals. The cone-shaped lid of the tajine captures steam and returns the condensed liquid to the pot. Therefore, a minimal

Tajine pots are used throughout North Africa.

Saffron and Raisin Couscous

Couscous is the Algerian national dish. It can be cooked with many different simple flavors added. Here's a version with saffron, raisins, and mint. Have an adult help you with this recipe.

Ingredients

2 cups water

½ teaspoon saffron

½ teaspoon olive oil

½ teaspoon salt

2 cups couscous

¼ cup raisins

3 tablespoons chopped fresh mint

Directions

Boil the water in a pan on the stovetop. Add the saffron, remove the pan from the heat, and let stand for 30 minutes. Put the pan back on the heat, return the water to a boil, and mix in the olive oil, salt, couscous, and raisins. Fluff the couscous with a fork, top it with fresh mint, and serve. This will make eight servings.

amount of water is needed to cook meats and vegetables, which is practical in a desert country with limited water supplies. Today, some cooks use electric tajines. Side dishes of meat, carrots, and chickpeas add flavor to the couscous. Two other Algerian dishes made with semolina wheat are the cakelike *basbousa* and *tamina*, which are roasted with butter and honey.

At home, tea with fresh mint is the most popular hot beverage. Algerians also drink strong coffee, often with a dash of cardamom. Gracious hosts generally offer a glass of orange blossom water with the coffee. Both adults and children love fruit

In Algeria, people typically drink tea out of glasses rather than cups.

Algerians share a meal at a celebration.

drinks of all kinds and *sharbats*, nut-flavored milk drinks. *Laban* is a mixture of yogurt and water that is flavored with mint leaves.

Some Berbers drink goat milk, while Tuaregs prefer a sweet, thick beverage called *eghajira*. This concoction consists of pounded millet, dates, and goat cheese mixed with water and eaten with a ladle. Algerians also enjoy soft drinks, consuming an average of 17 gallons (64 L) per person each year.

A typical breakfast treat is *m'shewsha*. This fried cake is made with eggs, a little semolina wheat, and some plain flour. Children pour warm honey over the cakes to sweeten them.

Whether prepared in a high-rise apartment or in a desert tent, sweets are Algerians' snack of choice. Principal ingre-

Playing Dominoes

Dominoes is a favorite game among Algerians. Men gather over tea with friends and neighbors for a match after the evening meal. In the old days, cafés used to rent game pieces. Today, most Algerians have their personal favorite set, and many teenagers compete online.

There are many versions of dominoes, with Flower & Scorpion evolving out of games brought to North Africa by French colonists. In this version, the two pairs of dice are colored red for the Scorpion set and green for the Flower set. Typically, when playing dominoes, the place where the dominoes are kept until being played is called the boneyard. But Flower & Scorpion uses the term *oasis* instead. A line of tiles is called a caravan, and the caravan master helps run the game.

dients are almonds, chocolate, and syrups. A silver tray of high-quality *deglet nour*, nicknamed the Queen of All the Dates, is always on hand. The best dates come from the oases of Tolga and M'Chouneche and are served naturally or stuffed with almond paste. Many Algerians are proud of their homemade rice pudding called *mhalbi*. *Bourek laajina*, a doughy fritter, is the Algerian version of what are called samosas elsewhere in the world. Also popular is an Algerian nougat from Constantine that is stuffed with nuts and sweetened with honey.

When rushing to music lessons or to play soccer, young people can buy a *brochette* for a quick snack. This sizzling chicken or beef kebab grilled on a skewer is found at food stalls in the souk, the town marketplace. All pig products, including pork, bacon, and ham, are not allowed under Islamic dietary rules.

The Algerian haik veil is traditionally white.

Clothing

In Algeria, work clothes range from rugged jeans to stylish suits to fancy dresses, depending on a person's job. In the dry, hot countryside, loose-fitting clothes are most comfortable. A traditional long outer garment for women is the *haik*. It is a veil-like fabric that covers a woman from head to toe. Beneath the haik, a woman wears loose-fitting trousers called *saroual*. Because of Muslim emphasis on modesty, Algerian women usually cover their heads with scarves. Yet beneath the scarves and veils, they often wear clothes in vibrant colors, with intricate designs made of gold and silver threads.

Traditional clothing for men includes a hooded woolen cloak called a *burnoose* or a long, loose gown called a *gandoura*.

Teens love the latest styles, including fancy sneakers and T-shirts printed with the names of their favorite sports teams.

A woman who has just graduated from a police academy celebrates with her mother.

Men and Women

In recent decades, women in Algeria have slowly gained more rights and freedom. More and more women have professional careers. About 20 percent of Algerian women now have jobs outside the home. The Algerian Network of Business Women gives voice to women's issues in the workplace. In 2013, Algerian entrepreneur Nadia Habes was awarded the prize

Khadija Benguenna, Journalist

Born in Algeria in 1965, Khadija Benguenna studied radio and television at the Media Institute at University of Algiers. Since 1997, she has been a news reporter for the Al Jazeera television network in the Middle Eastern country of Qatar. She has received many awards for her courageous coverage of political corruption and social issues in North Africa and the Middle East.

Getting Married

Young Algerians can marry whomever they wish. Parents, however, often have a say in the arrangement, and sometimes use a professional matchmaker.

The groom's mother checks out the prospective bride's family to be sure the marriage will be a suitable match. Marriage in Algeria is considered to be not just the union of two people, but also of two families. If the woman's character is approved, the man's family approaches her family to propose marriage. If all goes according to plan, the couple goes to the mosque for their formal engagement. These rituals are hundreds of years old.

After the engagement, there is much scurrying around to purchase things with which to start a new home, including household items and clothes. This is called *shoura*. Families are proud of the amount of money spent on a wedding. More is considered better because it demonstrates how generous they are. Wedding celebrations last for days, with music and ritual baths for the bride. The groom covers the costs of the festivities.

After the wedding meal, the bride is taken to the groom's house. She is seated in a comfortable chair and the guests sing and dance around her, saying farewell.

for best business leader at the World Forum of Women Heads of Business. Many Algerian women also have jobs based at home, such as farming, livestock management, and weaving.

Women are also being heard from more and more on the political front. About 31 percent of the members of the national legislature are women. There are at least four women generals. Algeria also has the largest number of female police officers in the Muslim world, with women making up 8 percent of its entire force.

Tuareg culture has more equality between men and women than other groups in Algeria. Women are in charge of managing the family money and property. Tuareg girls are allowed to have boyfriends before marrying. Both boys and girls are encouraged to attend school. The Tuareg are great storytellers and have many tales about their female ancestors. One recalls the warrior Tagurmat whose twin daughters were said to be the first herbal healers.

Coming to Visit

Algeria has a lot to offer visitors. The country invites tourists to enjoy its food, ceremonies, museums, ancient ruins, mountains, and beaches. The country is also hoping to increase its convention and trade show business. The long list of events hosted in Algeria include the annual Alger Fashion Fair and a major Medical and Hospital Equipment International Expo.

Ethnic Algerian-French citizens make up the largest number of guests to the country, followed by Tunisians. The country has ambitious plans to develop its potential. The Ministry of Tourism expects visitor numbers to rise to 3.1 million by 2023 from the 2.6 million estimated in 2013. It's only a matter of time. In Algeria, the door is always open.

Timeline

ALGERIAN HISTORY

People begin making art on cliff walls at Tassili n'Ajjer.	**ca. 8000 BCE**
The climate of North Africa becomes much drier.	**ca. 2000 BCE**
Phoenicians establish outposts in what is now Algeria.	**ca. 1100 BCE**
Carthaginian influence extends over the region.	**800s BCE**
Rome conquers the Berber Numidian kingdom.	**105 BCE**
Vandals invade North Africa.	**429 CE**
Byzantines defeat the Vandals.	**534**
Arab Muslims sweep into North Africa.	**600s**
The Rustamid dynasty, Algeria's first Muslim state, is founded.	**777**
The Ottoman Turks gain control of the region.	**Early 1500s**
Pirates control the North African coast.	**1500s–1800s**

WORLD HISTORY

ca. 2500 BCE	The Egyptians build the pyramids and the Sphinx in Giza.
ca. 563 BCE	The Buddha is born in India.
313 CE	The Roman emperor Constantine legalizes Christianity.
610	The Prophet Muhammad begins preaching a new religion called Islam.
1054	The Eastern (Orthodox) and Western (Roman Catholic) Churches break apart.
1095	The Crusades begin.
1215	King John seals the Magna Carta.
1300s	The Renaissance begins in Italy.
1347	The plague sweeps through Europe.
1453	Ottoman Turks capture Constantinople, conquering the Byzantine Empire.
1492	Columbus arrives in North America.
1500s	Reformers break away from the Catholic Church, and Protestantism is born.
1776	The U.S. Declaration of Independence is signed.
1789	The French Revolution begins.

ALGERIAN HISTORY		WORLD HISTORY
The Second Barbary War concludes.	**1815**	
France invades Algeria.	**1830**	
Algeria becomes part of France.	**1848**	
	1865	The American Civil War ends.
	1879	The first practical lightbulb is invented.
	1914	World War I begins.
	1917	The Bolshevik Revolution brings communism to Russia.
	1929	A worldwide economic depression begins.
Allied troops invade Algeria during World War II.	**1942** **1939**	World War II begins.
	1945	World War II ends.
The Algerian revolution begins.	**1954**	
Oil is discovered at Hassi Messaoud.	**1956**	
Algeria wins independence from France.	**1962**	
Algeria nationalizes oil companies.	**1971** **1969**	Humans land on the Moon.
An earthquake kills 5,000 people.	**1980** **1975**	The Vietnam War ends.
Riots result in economic reforms and a new constitution.	**1988** **1989**	The Berlin Wall is torn down as communism crumbles in Eastern Europe.
Civil war in Algeria results in 150,000 deaths.	**1990s** **1991**	The Soviet Union breaks into separate states.
	2001	Terrorists attack the World Trade Center in New York City and the Pentagon near Washington, D.C.
	2004	A tsunami in the Indian Ocean destroys coastlines in Africa, India, and Southeast Asia.
Algerians approve a peace plan that pardons extremists.	**2005** **2008**	The United States elects Barack Obama its first African American president.
President Abdelaziz Bouteflika is elected to a fourth term.	**2014**	
Tamazight becomes an official language of Algeria.	**2016**	

Fast Facts

Official name: People's Democratic Republic of Algeria

Capital: Algiers

Official languages: Arabic, Tamazight

Oran

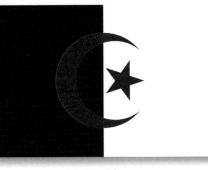

National flag

Official religion:	Islam
National anthem:	"Kassaman" ("We pledge")
Type of government:	Republic
Head of state:	President
Head of government:	Prime Minister
Total area:	919,595 square miles (2,381,740 sq km)
Bordering countries:	Morocco, Western Sahara, and Mauritania to the west; Mali and Niger to the south; Libya and Tunisia to the east.
Length of coastline:	620 miles (1,000 km)
Lowest elevation:	Chott Melrhir, 131 feet (40 m) below sea level
Highest elevation:	Mount Tahat, 9,850 feet (3,002 m) above sea level
Longest river:	Chelif, 450 miles (725 km)
Average daily high temperature:	In Algiers, 62°F (17°C) in January, 90°F (32°C) in July; in Reggane, 73°F (23°C) in January, 116°F (47°C) in July
Average daily low temperature:	In Algiers, 42°F (6°C) in January, 67°F (19°C) in July; in Reggane, 49°F (9°C) in January, 91°F (33°C) in July
Average annual precipitation:	8 to 16 inches (20 to 40 cm); less than 5 inches (13 cm) in the Sahara

Sahara Desert

Algiers

Currency

National population (2016 est.):	40,407,913	
Population of largest cities:	Algiers	2,364,230
	Oran	893,329
	Constantine	448,028
	Annaba	342,793
	Blida	331,779

Landmarks:
- ▶ *Belezma National Park*
- ▶ *Demaeght Museum*, Oran
- ▶ *Grand Mosque minaret*, Algiers
- ▶ *Kasbah*, Algiers
- ▶ *Palace of Ahmed Bey*, Constantine

Economy: Oil and gas are the mainstays of Algeria's economy, accounting for 95 percent of the country's export revenues. The country has an estimated twelve billion barrels of oil reserves and produces about 1.2 million barrels a day. Algeria is Africa's largest producer of natural gas and has the tenth-largest reserves in the world. The country's natural resources include salt, crushed stone, dolomite, feldspar, gypsum, lime, limestone, marble, nitrogen, quartzite, sand and gravel, and sulfur. Algeria also manufactures steel and cement. It exports wine, dates, and olives.

Currency: The dinar. In 2016, 109 dinars equaled US$1.

System of weights and measures: Metric system

Literacy rate: 73%

Soccer

Taoufik Makhloufi

Common Tamazight words and phrases:

Axir	Hello
Sbah Ixir	Good morning
Mxelxir	Good evening
Ggiyak lehna	Good-bye

Prominent Algerians:

Augustine (354–430)
Christian philosopher

Ahmed Ben Bella (ca. 1919–2012)
President

Hassiba Boulmerka (1968–)
Runner and Olympic medalist

Albert Camus (1913–1960)
Nobel Prize-winning author

Claude Cohen-Tannoudji (1933–)
Nobel Prize–winning physicist

Cheb Khaled (1960–)
Singer and musician

Taoufik Makhloufi (1988–)
Runner and Olympic medalist

Abd al-Qadir (1808–1883)
Revolutionary leader

To Find Out More

Books

- Guène, Faïza. *Kiffe Kiffe Tomorrow.* New York: Mariner Books, 2006.

- Kilmeade, Brian, and Don Yaeger. *Thomas Jefferson and the Tripoli Pirates: The Forgotten War That Changed American History.* New York: Sentinel Publishing, 2015.

- Marston, Elsa. *The Compassionate Warrior: Abd el-Kader of Algeria.* Bloomington, IN: Wisdom Tales, 2013.

Music

- *Algerian Berber Music.* Washington, DC: Smithsonian Folkways, 2004.

- *Arabic Groove.* New York: Putumayo World Music, 2001.

- Khaled. *Sahra.* New York: Island Records, 1997.

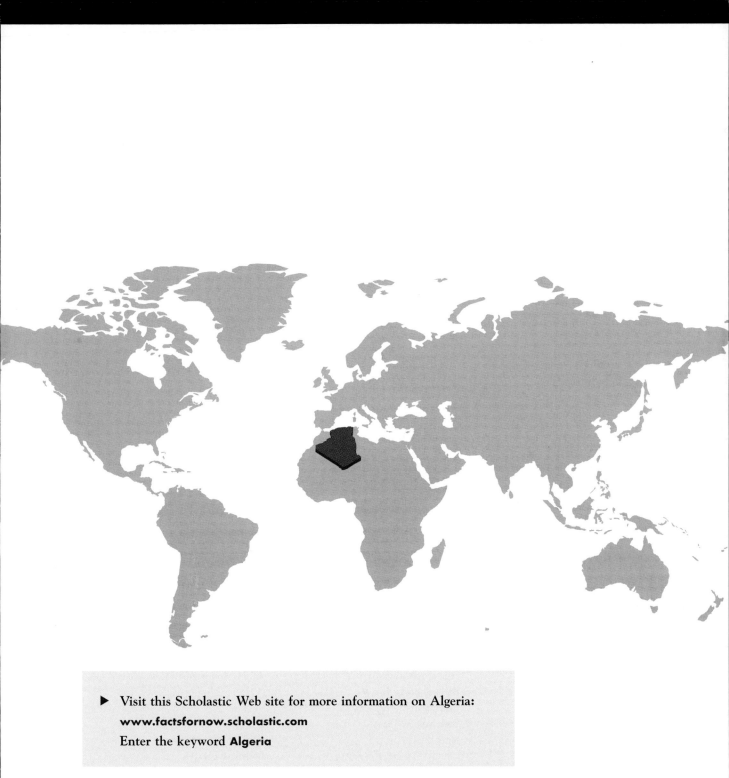

▶ Visit this Scholastic Web site for more information on Algeria:
www.factsfornow.scholastic.com
Enter the keyword **Algeria**

Index

Page numbers in *italics*
indicate illustrations.

Meet the Author

MARTIN HINTZ HAS WRITTEN MORE than one hundred books for young readers and adults, including many volumes for the Enchantment of the World series. He has written on all kinds of topics, from cheese to training elephants to motorcycle racing.

A longtime journalist, Hintz publishes *The Irish American Post*, an online magazine covering Irish and Irish American affairs. Hintz also writes articles for other publications, covering film and entertainment, agricultural issues, and ethnic affairs.

Hintz is a board member of the Milwaukee Press Club Endowment, has served as president of the Society of American Travel Writers, and belongs to other journalism organizations. As director of Buffalo Stampede Productions, Hintz writes film scripts and consults on cinema projects.

Hintz and his wife, Pam Percy, live on a farm in Wisconsin. They raise chickens, goats, hogs, and rabbits. They also grow produce, host farm-to-table dinners, and run a kids' camp on the farm each summer.

Photo Credits

Photographs ©:

cover: frans lemmens/Alamy Images; back cover: Melba/age fotostock; 2: Mehdi33300/Thinkstock; 5: GIUGLIO Gil/Getty Images; 6 left: Andia/Getty Images; 6 center: Universal Images Group North America LLC/DeAgostini/Alamy Images; 6 right: Jeremy Woodhouse/Blend Images/Superstock, Inc.; 7 left: Michael Runkel/imageBROKER/age fotostock; 7 right: Yann Arthus-Bertrand/Getty Images; 8: BSIP SA/Alamy Images; 11: José Fuste Raga/age fotostock; 12: frans lemmens/Alamy Images; 13: De Agostini/G. Dagli Orti/Getty Images; 14: Egmont Strigl/imageBROKER/age fotostock; 17: Andia/Getty Images; 18: De Agostini/Archivio J. Lange/age fotostock; 19: Martin Ruegner/Media Bakery; 20 top: Ivan Vdovin/Alamy Images; 20 bottom: Feije Riemersma/Alamy Images; 21: Universal Images Group North America LLC/DeAgostini/Alamy Images; 22: Yann Arthus-Bertrand/Getty Images; 23 bottom: Nick Laing/Getty Images; 23 top: muha04/iStockphoto; 24: FAYEZ NURELDINE/Getty Images; 25 top: Peter Giovannini/imageBROKER/age fotostock; 25 bottom: REUTERS/Alamy Images; 26: Michael Runkel/age fotostock; 28: Biosphoto/Superstock, Inc.; 29: F. Teigler/age fotostock; 30: D Assmann/age fotostock; 31 top: Egmont Strigl/imageBROKER/age fotostock; 31 bottom: Adam Jones/Getty Images; 32: JUNIORS BILDARCHIV/age fotostock; 33: Jeremy Woodhouse/Blend Images/Superstock, Inc.; 34: imagesandstories/age fotostock; 35: Hemis/Alamy Images; 36: Brother Luck/Alamy Images; 38: MAISANT Ludovic/hemis.fr/Getty Images; 40 top: Sarin Images/The Granger Collection; 41: DEA/C. SAPPA/Getty Images; 42: Pantheon/Superstock, Inc.; 44: GL Archive/Alamy Images; 45: Roger-Viollet/The Image Works; 46 top: DEA/M. SEEMULLER/Getty Images; 47: Daily Herald Archive/National Media Museum/SSP/Science and Society/Superstock, Inc.; 48: ASSOCIATED PRESS/AP Images; 50: Stringer/Getty Images; 51: REUTERS/Alamy Images; 52: Nacerdine ZEBAR/Getty Images; 53: AFP/Getty Images; 54: FAYEZ NURELDINE/Getty Images; 57: Popow/ullstein bild/The Image Works; 58: AFP/Getty Images; 59: camelt/iStockphoto; 60: FAYEZ NURELDINE/Getty Images; 61: FAYEZ NURELDINE/Getty Images; 62: REUTERS/Alamy Images; 63 top right: Hemis/Alamy Images; 63 bottom right: De Agostini/C. Sappa/Getty Images; 64: Pascal Parrot/Getty Images; 66: PAGES Francois/Getty Images; 67: FAROUK BATICHE/Getty Images; 68: Peter Jordan/Alamy Images; 69: ton koene/Alamy Images; 71: REUTERS/Alamy Images; 72: Universal Images Group North America LLC/DeAgostini/Alamy Images; 74 top: OUAHAB HEBBAT/AP Images; 74 bottom: Ivan Vdovin/age fotostock; 75: GFC Collection/Alamy Images; 76: frans lemmens/Alamy Images; 78: Ted Pink/Alamy Images; 80 bottom: Xinhua/Alamy Images; 81: Michael Runkel/imageBROKER/age fotostock; 82: Godong/Alamy Images; 83: robertharding/Alamy Images; 84: William STEVENS/Alamy Images; 85: Yann Arthus-Bertrand/Getty Images; 87: Godong/age fotostock; 88: epa european pressphoto agency b.v./Alamy Images; 89: Patrick Durand/Getty Images; 90: FAROUK BATICHE/Getty Images; 92: Lanmas/Alamy Images; 93: Reza/Getty Images; 94: Anadolu Agency/Getty Images; 96: Art Directors & TRIP/Alamy Images; 97: Albert Harlingue/Roger-Viollet/The Image Works; 98: epa european pressphoto agency b.v./Alamy Images; 99: Sébastien CAILLEUX/Getty Images; 100: REUTERS/Alamy Images; 101: AFP/Getty Images; 102: frans lemmens/Alamy Images; 104: DEA/G DAGLI ORTI/age fotostock; 105: ASK Images/Alamy Images; 106: REUTERS/Alamy Images; 107: Erick Nguyen/Alamy Images; 108: REUTERS/Alamy Images; 109: REUTERS/Alamy Images; 110 left: ASSOCIATED PRESS/AP Images; 110 right: Ulf Andersen/SIPA/AP Images; 111: CASBAH/IGOR/Album; 113: Roger-Viollet/The Image Works; 114: FAYEZ NURELDINE/Getty Images; 115: Jae C. Hong/AP Images; 116: Photononstop/Superstock, Inc.; 118: KAUFFMANN Alain/hem/age fotostock; 119: Jan Wlodarczyk/Alamy Images; 120: CSP_vanillaechoes/age fotostock; 121: FAROUK BATICHE/Getty Images; 122: Reza/Getty Images; 123: Charles Stirling (Travel)/Alamy Images; 124: epa european pressphoto agency b.v./Alamy Images; 125: REUTERS/Alamy Images; 126: FAYEZ NURELDINE/Getty Images; 130 left: Nick Laing/Getty Images; 131 top: camelt/iStockphoto; 131 bottom: BSIP SA/Alamy Images; 132 bottom: Ivan Vdovin/age fotostock; 132 top: Hemis/Alamy Images; 133 top: FAYEZ NURELDINE/Getty Images; 133 bottom: Jae C. Hong/AP Images.

Maps by Mapping Specialists.